WHERE ARCHITECTS STAY IN GERMANY

LODGINGS
FOR
DESIGN
ENTHUSIASTS

SIBYLLE KRAMER

WHERE ARCHITECTS STAY IN GERMANY

LODGINGS
FOR
DESIGN
ENTHUSIASTS

BRAUN

The Deutsche Nationalbibliothek lists this
publication in the Deutsche Nationalbib-
liografie; detailed bibliographic data are
available on the Internet at http://dnb.dnb.de

ISBN 978-3-03768-255-5
© 2020 by Braun Publishing AG
www.braun-publishing.ch

1st edition 2020

Editor: Sibylle Kramer
Editorial staff and layout:
María Barrera del Amo, Alessia Calabrò
Translation: Sandra Ellegiers
Graphic concept: Michaela Prinz, Berlin
Reproduction: Bild1Druck GmbH, Berlin

Contents

Contents

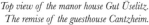
Top view of the manor house Gut Üselitz.
The remise of the guesthouse Cantzheim.

Preface

Architecture and vacation is a promising combination. Perfect surroundings for recreation and delight fulfill almost every wish.

After the success of the first volumes "Where Architects Stay" and "Where Architects Stay in Europe", this new volume focusing on Germany meets the readers' demands for a geographically concentrated travel guide by presenting 52 new, particularly charming examples of architectural accommodations in Germany.

It is usually the stories and concepts that make these small and fine lodgings so special. There are beloved houses that have been family owned for generations and are saved from distinction by being converted into a holiday home, such as the Pflughof, a farmhouse which has been transformed into a unique property by the owners and Sutter3 KG studio. The wild, historical character of the listed building can still be experienced, old and new form an exciting symbiosis, rough and caring at the same time. Or the buildings are enchanted and fallen into disrepair, but brought to life again by the dreams and courage of their founders, as Gut Üselitz on Rügen recalls. The 16th-century manor house was awakened from its slumber by its current owners and the office of Pete J.C. Welbergen, Clara Welbergen. Beside the romantic refuges in the beautiful countryside, by the lake or in the mountains, urban new and old buildings with sophisticated designs

*Interior view of a bedroom from the
Flushing Meadows. Exterior view
of the Kapitänshaus Wieck.
Atelier space from Moosham 13.*

attract visitors to stay overnight as well. For example, with its exceptional apartment concept the Nomads is a generous and cosmopolitan host – an invitation to dance, make music and also an oasis of peace. Moreover, the metropolitan and sensual design of the rooms promises memorable Berlin nights.

All these architecturally consistently designed accommodations and well-conceived concepts are based on the passion of their creators. Guests benefit from the mixture of high-quality architecture, individual history and very special location.

Experience Germany from its esthetic, individual, historical, exciting and surprising side: whether in a former water tower, in a tree house or in a big-city apartment. Travel and immerse yourself in a unique accommodation with an idyllic and inspiring atmosphere.

INFORMATION. ARCHITECTS>
WIRTH ALONSO ARCHITEKTEN // 2017.
HOLIDAY HOME> 130 SQM // 8 GUESTS
// 3 BEDROOMS // 2 BATHROOMS +
1 WC. ADDRESS> WERDERSCHER
DAMM 5, POTSDAM, BRANDENBURG.
WWW.WASSERTURM.HOLIDAY

Wasserturm am Park Sanssouci

POTSDAM, BRANDENBURG

Originally, the 100-year-old water tower was used to supply steam locomotives with water. After the introduction of electric and diesel locomotives, it was no longer used and visibly deteriorated. A German-Spanish couple of architects took over the ruins and converted the tower into a six-story holiday apartment plus roof terrace. The aim of the renovation was to make the ascent an experience and at the same time to preserve as much of the old substance as possible. On the ground floor a large table under the brick cupola invites to cozy evenings. Upstairs there are three sleeping levels with bathrooms. This is followed by the room of the tower history with its original fittings. Abstraction and geometric order dominate the living room in the former water tank on the top floor. A large window in the riveted wall of the water tank provides a view over the game park. Following the vertical reading of the building, it ends on a roof terrace with a 360° panoramic view over the trees, covered by the steel skeleton of the former roof. The white furnishings underline the industrial architecture of red brickwork and anthracite steel. The open living space offers a wide range of visual impressions and makes the round shape of the tower palpable everywhere.

Interior view of the kitchen. Second floor. Staircase. General view from the game park.

11

*Living room in the former water tank. Detail of
the bathroom. Staircase from below. Vertical cross
section.*

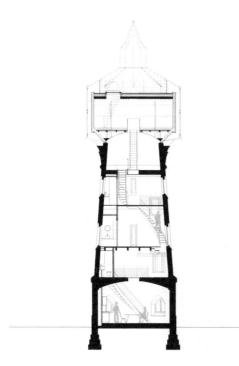

GETTING AROUND. THE WATER
TOWER BORDERS THE GAME PARK
AND IS ONLY A FEW MINUTES WALK
AWAY FROM THE PARK SANSSOUCI.
THE PARK'S RAILWAY STATION IS
ALSO VERY CLOSE BY. YOU CAN
REACH THE CENTER OF BERLIN BY
TRAIN IN JUST 30 MINUTES. WITH ITS
NUMEROUS MONUMENTS THE CITY
OF POTSDAM ITSELF HAS A LOT
TO OFFER. BUT ABOVE ALL, THE
IMMEDIATE AREA INVITES TO WALKS
THROUGH THE GAME PARK, BICYCLE
TOURS AND EXCURSIONS TO THE
MANY BATHING LAKES.

One of the bedrooms. Roof terrace.

INFORMATION. ARCHITECTS>
HÜTTNER ARCHITEKTEN // 2017.
HOTEL> 1,540 SQM // 47 GUESTS //
28 BEDROOMS // 28 BATHROOMS.
ADDRESS> LUITPOLDSTRASSE 10,
HELMBRECHTS, BAVARIA.
WWW.VILLA-WEISS.DE

Hotel VILLA WEISS

HELMBRECHTS, BAVARIA

VILLA WEISS is situated close to nature between the Frankenwald forests and the mountains of the Fichtelgebirge in the center of the small town of Helmbrechts, in the most northern part of Bavaria. The listed former industrialist's villa, whose origins date back to the 17th century, was renovated and converted into a boutique hotel with 28 guest beds. The building is characterized by its historical structure, modern design and a harmonic color concept with natural materials. The house offers ideal conditions for music courses and ensembles with a grand piano, sound-insulated practice rooms and a seminar rooms. In 1880, the main building was overbuilt, and since then its neoclassical façade shapes the townscape. The ground floor contains the Wedding Room. It had been converted into a lavish neoclassical-sizistic style as a bridal gift to the daughter of the former landlord, and is now used as a concert hall, seminar room or wedding room. A wellness area has been set up in the vaulted basement. The transept above the baroque stables now houses a breakfast room and a room with fireplace, overlooking the courtyard and garden. The former barn building located under the mighty lime tree in the rear garden has been replaced by a new building with guest rooms and seminar room.

A bedroom. Exterior view of the Hotel VILLA WEISS. Event space. Interior view of a room.

View of the bistro. The new seminar room.
A bedroom. Floor plan. Suite with bathtub.

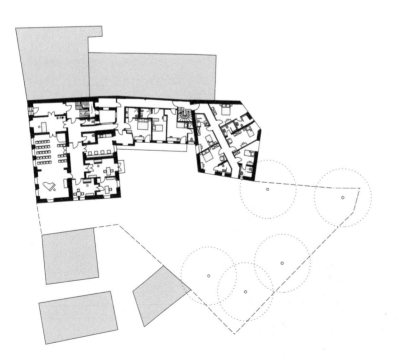

GETTING AROUND. HELMBRECHTS, ONCE A HUB FOR THE TEXTILE AND PLASTICS INDUSTRY, IS ABOUT HALF AN HOUR AWAY FROM HOF. THE TEXTIL MUSEUM OF OBERFRANKEN (UPPER FRANCONIA) IS ONLY FIVE MINUTES AWAY FROM THE WEISSE VILLA. THE KIRCHBERG MOUNTAIN IS ALSO JUST A COUPLE OF MINUTES AWAY FROM THE HOTEL, OFFERING A WONDERFUL VIEW OF THE COUNTRYSIDE. NUMEROUS MARKED CIRCULAR HIKING TRAILS LEAD TO CHARMING LANDSCAPES.

INFORMATION. ARCHITECTS>
GROTHEER ARCHITEKTUR // 2016.
REED ROOF HOUSE WITH TWO
APARTMENTS > APPROX. 203 SQM //
6 GUESTS APARTMENT WEST,
4 GUESTS APARTMENT EAST //
3 BEDROOMS APARTMENT WEST,
2 BEDROOMS APARTMENT EAST //
2 BATHROOMS + 1 WC APARTMENT
WEST, 1 BATHROOM + 1 WC
APARTMENT EAST. ADDRESS>
KERTELHEINALLEE 12, NIEBLUM IN
FÖHR, SCHLESWIG-HOLSTEIN.
WWW.STEUERMANN.HAUS

Living room of apartment West. Interior view of apartment East. Kitchen and dining area - apartment West. West view from the street.

Haus Steuermann

NIEBLUM IN FÖHR,
SCHLESWIG-HOLSTEIN

You will find Haus Steuermann in the village Nieblum, on the North Frisian Island Föhr, the so-called green island, in the lee of Amrum and Sylt. The white reed roof house was built in 1814 and has been used since then by farmers and bakers, sailors and students. Since 2016 it accommodates holiday guests, who find here the purity of the old building substance. There are modern design classics, custom-made fittings and first-class furnishings at both wings of the carefully and with high quality standards restored house. The room is white with pastel details and lightwood giving a fresh and clean atmosfere. The luxurious holiday home is divided into Helmsman West and Helmsman East. The Helmsman West can accommodate six people on two floors and 120 square meters. The beds are located in three rooms: Two with a double bed and one with two single beds. On the ground floor there is a loft-like living and kitchen area with fireplace and a bedroom with en-suite bathroom. On the first floor there are two more bedrooms and a glas sauna.

The East Helmsman can accommodate four people on two floors and 92 square meters. The beds are in two bedrooms: one room with a double bed and one room with two single beds. On the ground floor there is a loft-like living and kitchen area with a tunnel fireplace and guest toilet. On the upper floor there are bedrooms and a large bathroom. Both houses have their own entrance, a large garden and two terraces.

Dining area with fireplace.
View from the garden.

Bedroom in the first floor. Interior view.
Floor plans.

GETTING AROUND. THE NORTH SEA ISLAND OF FÖHR IS SURROUNDED BY THE WADDEN SEA, A WORLD HERITAGE SITE, AND HAS RETAINED ITS OLD NORTH FRISIAN CHARM TO THE PRESENT DAY. NIEBLUM IS REGARDED AS THE MOST BEAUTIFUL VILLAGE ON THE ISLAND AND IS FAMOUS FOR ITS WONDERFUL REED-COVERED CAPTAIN'S HOUSES AND ITS BEAUTIFUL MEDIEVAL CHURCH OF ST. JOHANNIS. HOUSE STEUERMANN IS LOCATED IN THE MIDDLE OF NIEBLUM ON A VILLAGE ROAD, SURROUNDED BY SUMMER LIME TREES AND HEDGE ROSES.

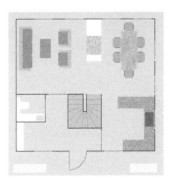

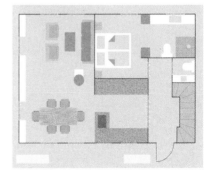

INFORMATION. ARCHITECTS>
BAUMRAUM, ANDREAS WENNING //
2016. TREE HOUSE CABINS> 30 SQM
PER CABIN + 18.4 SQM TERRACE //
2 GUESTS // 1 BEDROOM // 1
BATHROOM. ADDRESS>
SCHANZENSTRASSE 23,
DROCHTERSEN-KRAUTSAND,
LOWER SAXONY.
WWW.ELBINSELHOF-KRAUTSAND.DE

Baumhaus — Hotel Elbinsel-hof Krautsand

DROCHTERSEN-KRAUTSAND, LOWER SAXONY

The history of the farm can be traced back to the 16th century. At that time eleven families settled on the island of the river Elbe and erected here the first mounds, the so-called Wurten. One of them still represents the basis of the farm to this day. This is where the hosts live and where the three tree houses on stilts are located, right next to the Elbe. The view from up here to the surrounding nature and its fauna is amazing. From this elevated place of recreation, not only the birds can be watched, but also the big ships that navigate on the Elbe to their next destination are fascinating. The interior of the comfortable tree houses is made of oak wood and contains binoculars, a bird identification book, a tide calendar and an iPad with a ship identification app. So there's no danger of getting bored in the cozy tree houses equipped with a wood-burning stove and alcove bed which gives a feeling of security in a welcoming atmosphere during a short break. The treehouses accommodate up to four people. The relaxation offer includes bathing in a hot pot as well as wellness treatment in the so-called Erdhaus (earth house), a 26 square metre room that can be used in many ways.

View from garden. Interior view of the alcove bed. Bathroom. Living and dining room with fireplace.

Dining room in the Erdhaus. Kitchen of the Erdhaus. Garden view of the Erdhaus. Floor plan of the tree house.

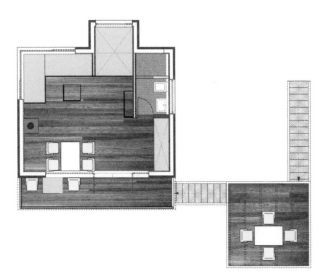

GETTING AROUND. THE LARGE BEACH INVITES TO EXTENSIVE WALKS OR RIDING IN A BEAUTIFUL SETTING AT THE RIVER ELBE. THE HORSES ARE STANDING ON THE HOUSE'S OWN PADDOCK. BUT ALSO THE SURROUNDINGS OFFER A LOT OF INTERESTING THINGS, FOR EXAMPLE A TRIP TO GLÜCKSTADT AT THE OTHER SIDE OF THE RIVER ELBE.

Evening atmosphere.
Interior view.

INFORMATION. ARCHITECTS>
GIORGIO GULLOTTA ARCHITEKTEN //
2019. HOTEL> ADDITIONAL ROOMS
APPROX. 1,800 SQM // 43 NEW ROOMS.
ADDRESS> SIMON-VON-UTRECHT-
STRASSE 31, HAMBURG.
WWW.EAST-HAMBURG.DE

Studio, suite. Detail. Loft.
Interior view of a studio.

East Hotel

HAMBURG

The East Design Hotel opened in 2004 in an old iron foundry in St. Pauli in Hamburg. Designed by the artist Jordan Mozer, the hotel features organic shapes and a couple of color highlights. GiorgioGullotta Architects finished the conversion of the open-plan offices, the former sports and spa area and the club area to a further 43 rooms in 2019. The existing rooms are characterized by an open floor plan concept that was taken up in the planning of the new premises. In contrast to classic hotel rooms, the East Hotel offers a free-standing washstand and an open shower. The washbasin is either made of natural stone or placed on top of a walnut board and represents an important design element of the room. The shower opens to the room and allows a view on the precious natural green stone on the walls, which was installed on the floor in combination with high quality black oak from the Vosges in a herringbone pattern. The black oiled oak wall surfaces with brass accents and several burnished mirror surfaces create a luxurious interior. This is complemented by carefully selected materials and fabrics that make the rooms unique and of high quality. The design concept is further enriched by a range of lighting options like free standing, wall-mounted and pendant lamps as well as indirect light strips. The built-in furniture designed by the architect makes each room one of a kind and guarantees a pleasant stay.

Interior view of a loft. Studio.
En-suite bathroom. Floor plans of the different
room types: suite studio, studio, suite loft.

GETTING AROUND. THE EAST
DESIGN HOTEL IS LOCATED IN THE
HEART OF THE DISTRICT OF ST. PAULI,
CLOSE TO THE REEPERBAHN STREET.
OTHER EXCURSION DESTINATIONS
SUCH AS HAFENCITY, THE HARBOUR,
THE RIVERS ELBE AND ALSTER, THE
PIERS (LANDUNGSBRÜCKEN), THE
FAMOUS HAMBURGER MICHEL
CHURCH, THE DOWNTOWN AREA
WITH NUMEROUS SHOPPING
OPPORTUNITIES, THE MILLERNTOR
STADIUM, THE SPIELBUDENPLATZ
SQUARE AND THE OPERETTENHAUS
THEATER ARE JUST A FEW MINUTES
WALK AWAY OR CAN BE QUICKLY
AND EASILY REACHED BY PUBLIC
TRANSPORT.

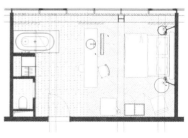

INFORMATION. ARCHITECTS> ALEX SCHWEDER, CLEMENS KLEIN // 2017. MANOR HOUSE> 780 SQM // 20 GUESTS // 10 BEDROOMS // 10 BATHROOMS. ADDRESS> GUTSHOF HESSENBURG DORFPLATZ 2–5, HESSENBURG / SAAL, MECKLENBURG-WESTERN POMERANIA WWW.KRANICHHOTEL.DE

Park view of the Kranich Museum & Hotel.
Interior view of the museum.
Living room with terrace – Apartment 2.

Kranich Museum & Hotel

HESSENBURG / SAAL, MECKLENBURG-WESTERN POMERANIA

The guests of the Kranich Museum & Hotel lodge in an 1840 manor house in the heartland of the cranes in the region of Mecklenburg-Vorpommern. The house suffered from the typical historic fate of the region. It used to be a farm house and then a "village community center" during the GDR era and suffered neglect after the fall of the Wall. The installation artist and representative of performance architecture Alex Schweder from New York brought it back to life as a Gesamtkunstwerk. Artists in residence worked on the house, carrying their artworks into the museum and the guests' hotel rooms. The contemporary history is captured on the raw walls with a keen sense of touch. The wooden ceilings have been replaced by visible reinforced concrete ones creating a contrast to the restored wing doors from the past.

A walkway made of soaped planks and removed from the walls leads through the hotel rooms and surrounds nest-like beds. The light, the view of the park and the crackling fire in the old stoves make the hectic pace of modern everyday life fade. The house invites to discover art and the place.

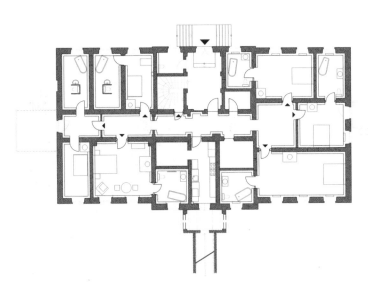

GETTING AROUND. THE KRANICH MUSEUM & HOTEL IS SITUATED IN A PARK OF 4.5 HA, ONLY 1 KM AWAY FROM THE SOUTHERN COAST OF THE BODDEN, A BIG INLAND LAKE. IN THE NORTH IT IS SURROUNDED BY THE PENINSULA FISCHLAND-DARSS-ZINGST AND THE BALTIC SEA. THE BEACH, BUT ALSO THE FAMOUS HANSEATIC CITIES OF ROSTOCK, STRALSUND, GRIFFSWALD, GÜSTROW AND WISMAR CAN BE REACHED WITHIN 30 TO 60 MINUTES. THE KRANICH CAFÉ WAS ESTABLISHED IN THE 250 YEAR OLD FORGE OF THE MANOR. CAKES AND DESSERTS ARE MADE IN SLOW FOOD STYLE. THE BUILDING CAN ALSO BE BOOKED FOR WEDDINGS AND OTHER OCCASIONS.

Evening mood. Floor plan. The Kranich Café in the old forge of the manor house.

Apartment 1. Light installation by Riccardo Giacconi – artist in residence 2017. Interior view of Apartment 6.

INFORMATION. ARCHITECTS>
SUTTER3 KG // 2017. HOLIDAY
APARTMENTS // 12 GUESTS //
6 BEDROOMS // 6 BATHROOMS.
ADDRESS> ALTE BUNDESSTRASSE 54 B,
GUNDELFINGEN, BAVARIA.
WWW.FRIZBNB.DE

*Lounge. Kitchen area. Interior view of one of the
apartments. Living room with designer furniture
and concrete wall.*

Pflughof

GUNDELFINGEN, BAVARIA

The barn is part of the agricultural domain Der Pflughof (founded in 1759), in the centre of Gundelfingen, Hochschwarzwald, one of only two domains still intact. At the domain, situated along the old Baden-Württemberg postal route, the family ran a guesthouse, one of five in a community of ninety souls. In 1843 Widow Arnold built the barn as stables for horses, oxen and cows. Sometimes the stables were occupied by Hussar regiments. In 1990, after nearly 250 years, farming activities were put on hold and the barn gradually fell into disrepair. With dedication and inspiration, after decades of neglect, the current owners, decided to reinstate and revive some of the domain's original identity by converting the barn into a contemporary dwelling with private and holiday apartments. In close collaboration with architectural planners Sutter3 KG, who specialise in projects involving listed buildings, both design professionals, created spaces, that are well designed and cleverly organised, using an articulated and balanced language of the modern (concrete) and the historic (beams, quarrystone). The outcome of this collaboration, with regard to the building's history, its architectural aspects and reinvention of its purpose, has been an absolute success.

Garden view by night.
Interior view. Living room.

A bedroom. Bathroom. Interior view.
Dining room. Longitudinal section.

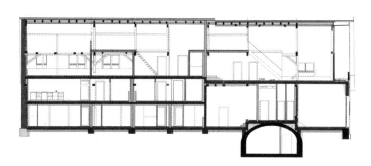

GETTING AROUND. THE PFLUGHOF IS
LOCATED IN GUNDELFINGEN AT THE
DANUBE RIVER, 5 KILOMETERS NORTH
OF FREIBURG IN BREISGAU. THE
SMALL BAVARIAN-SWABIAN TOWN
WITH ITS MEDIEVAL CORE INVITES YOU
TO TAKE A STROLL IN ITS IMMEDIATE
SURROUNDINGS, BUT IT IS LIKEWISE A
GOOD STARTING POINT FOR A TRIP
TO THE CITIES OF STRASBOURG
(90 KM) OR ZURICH (140 KM).

INFORMATION. ARCHITECTS>
MÖHRING ARCHITEKTEN BERLIN //
2018. HOLIDAY HOME> 178 SQM //
6 GUESTS // 3 BEDROOMS //
2 BATHROOMS. ADDRESS>
BLIESENRADER WEG 9, WIECK
A. DARSS, MECKLENBURG-
WESTERN POMERANIA.
WWW.QUARTIER-WIECK.DE

*Interior view of the kitchen and
dining room. View from the garden.
Exterior view.*

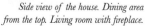

Side view of the house. Dining area from the top. Living room with fireplace.

Quartier-Wieck

WIECK A. DARSS,
MECKLENBURG-WESTERN
POMERANIA

The modern holiday home with a black wooden façade has been built in the former apple orchard in the small village of Wieck on the Darss, at the Baltic Sea. The reduced formal language of the angled house with its black, vertically scaled wooden formwork interacts with the copper roof. The result is an exciting interaction of shadow and light on the surfaces, which are not immune to the weather but become part of the aesthetics.

The window openings and the skylight create a light-flooded central room with kitchen and dining area and a living room with fireplace which is kept darker to allow the guests to retreat. The materials used in the interior with shell limestone, oak and stainless steel of the kitchen worktop show fissures in the surface and thus allow the viewer to constantly gain new exciting impressions.

As the owners traveled through Japan and Scandinavia, both Japanese and Nordic aesthetics find expression in the design of the building and its interior: minimalism, shadow play and the idea of Wabi-Sabi. There is beauty in the imperfection. Two works by Finnish contemporary artists from the owners' private collection are shown: Sami Lukkarinen and Petri Niemelä.

Exterior view from the garden. Living room.

Bedroom in the first floor. Wooden façade and copper roof. Floor plans.

GETTING AROUND. THE LITTLE VILLAGE OF WIECK ON THE DARSS IS THE PERFECT STARTING POINT FOR BEAUTIFUL TRIPS TO THE NATURE OR TO THE CLOSE OLD HANSEATIC TOWNS OF ROSTOCK OR STRALSUND. YOU CAN UNDERTAKE MANY SPORTING ACTIVITIES STARTING DIRECTLY FROM THE PROPERTY. THE HOLIDAY HOME IS ONLY 300 M FROM THE BODDEN BAY. THE SURROUNDINGS OF THE NATIONAL PARK ARE GREAT FOR CYCLISTS. GO TO THE BEACH FOR A SWIM OR TO THE LIGHTHOUSE DARSSER ORT. THE NETWORK OF CYCLE ROADS IS VERY WELL DEVELOPED AND QUITE LARGE. THE WESTERN BEACH - FROM AHRENSHOOP TO PREROW - IS ONE OF THE MOST BEAUTIFUL BEACHES IN THE WORLD. BEACH, WAVES AND ONLY NATURE.

INFORMATION. ARCHITECTS>
SILKE LORENZEN, SARAH VOLLMER //
2011. CARAVAN HOTEL IN A
FACTORY> 994.05 SQM // 43 GUESTS
// 18 BEDROOMS // 10 BATHROOMS.
ADDRESS> HOBRECHTSTRASSE 65/66,
BERLIN.
WWW.HUETTENPALAST.DE

Hüttenpalast

BERLIN

The founders of the Hüttenpalast Silke Lorenzen & Sarah Vollmer have been living in Berlin Neukölln for almost 20 years and decided in 2010 to shape their home neighborhood. The basic idea was to create a place where visitors to Berlin could already feel and experience a piece of the local Neukölln culture in their hotel. A backyard factory, that represents the typical architecture of Berlin, was the right place for the project. In May 2011, the Hüttenpalast hotel opened after a one-year construction period. The café with reception, the courtyard gardens and three overnight accommodation areas are located on almost 1,000 square meter: Hall 1 with three caravans, three wooden huts and two gender-separated shared bathrooms, Hall 2 with five caravans, a plateau, a separate lounge and two gender-separated shared bathrooms and the third area with six hotel rooms in factory loftstyle with en-suite bathrooms. The room-in-room concept provides a unique experience. Each car and each cabin has been individually designed with the help of local craftsmen and artists. The guests appreciate the personal and friendly style of the hotel as well as the 100-year history that the hotel embodies with the building, the vintage caravans and the interior design.

Sleeping room "Puck" caravan. "Berghütte".
Hall Two. View of the caravans.

Hotel room. Caravan "Kleine Schwester". "Alter Palast". Floor plans of the halls and hotel rooms.

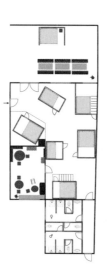

GETTING AROUND. BERLIN FASCINATES BY ITS EXTRAORDINARY RICHNESS OF SIGHTS, A DIVERSE CULTURAL LIFE AND A VIBRANT AND AT THE SAME TIME RELAXED LIFESTYLE. THE HOTEL IS LOCATED IN THE CENTRAL PART OF THE CITY, IN BUSTLING NEUKÖLLN. ANY DESTINATION CAN BE EASILY REACHED BY UNDERGROUND OR BICYCLE.

View towards hall 2. Sleeping area "Kleine Schwester".

INFORMATION. ARCHITECTS>
JUREK BRÜGGEN ARCH BSC ETH +
SEBASTIAN SAILER, KOSA
ARCHITEKTEN // 2018. HOLIDAY
HOME> 85–170 SQM // 2 GUESTS //
1 BEDROOM // 1 BATHROOM,
2 SEPARATE WC. ADDRESS>
AM MÜHLENBERG 21, WERDER,
BRANDENBURG.
WWW.FERIEN-WERDER.DE

Haus am See

WERDER, BRANDENBURG

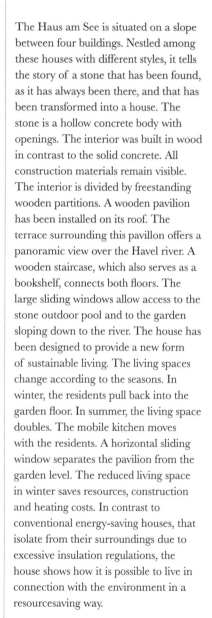

The Haus am See is situated on a slope between four buildings. Nestled among these houses with different styles, it tells the story of a stone that has been found, as it has always been there, and that has been transformed into a house. The stone is a hollow concrete body with openings. The interior was built in wood in contrast to the solid concrete. All construction materials remain visible. The interior is divided by freestanding wooden partitions. A wooden pavilion has been installed on its roof. The terrace surrounding this pavillon offers a panoramic view over the Havel river. A wooden staircase, which also serves as a bookshelf, connects both floors. The large sliding windows allow access to the stone outdoor pool and to the garden sloping down to the river. The house has been designed to provide a new form of sustainable living. The living spaces change according to the seasons. In winter, the residents pull back into the garden floor. In summer, the living space doubles. The mobile kitchen moves with the residents. A horizontal sliding window separates the pavilion from the garden level. The reduced living space in winter saves resources, construction and heating costs. In contrast to conventional energy-saving houses, that isolate from their surroundings due to excessive insulation regulations, the house shows how it is possible to live in connection with the environment in a resourcesaving way.

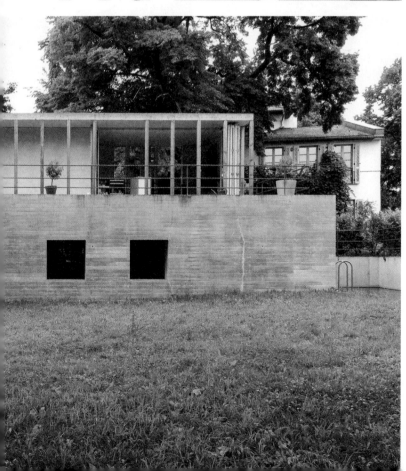

Dining area in the living room. Living room. Interior view of the pavilion. View from the garden.

West elevation of the house. Bathroom. View from the garden. Floor plans in the Summer. Bedroom.

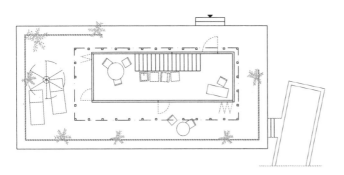

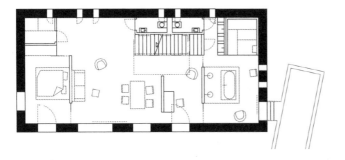

GETTING AROUND. THE HAUS AM SEE IS LOCATED ONLY 35 KM SOUTHWEST OF BERLIN, ON THE HIGHEST AND MOST BEAUTIFUL POINT OF THE ISLAND TOWN OF WERDER. THE EXTENSIVE PLOT OF LAND BORDERS THE ISLAND CHURCH AND STRETCHES DOWN TO THE BANKS OF THE HAVEL. THE ISLAND WERDER IS SURROUNDED BY A MULTIFACETED RIVER LANDSCAPE. THE HISTORIC CITY CENTRE IS UNDER PRESERVATION ORDER AND HAS BEEN LOVINGLY RESTORED. THE NOVELIST THEODOR FONTANE DESCRIBED THE ISLAND WERDER IN HIS "WANDERUNGEN DURCH DIE MARK BRANDENBURG" (WANDERINGS THROUGH THE MARK OF BRANDBURG) AS AN IMPRESSIVE REGION OF THE HAVELLAND.

INFORMATION. ARCHITECTS>
STEPHEN WILLIAMS, DAVID
CHIPPERFIELD, BERND LEUSMANN,
KATE HUME, JOYCE WANG // 2018.
HOTEL> 8,500 SQM // 252 GUESTS //
126 BEDROOMS // 126 BATHROOMS.
ADDRESS> STADTHAUSBRÜCKE 10,
HAMBURG.
WWW.TORTUE.DE

Lobby. Bar Noir. View from the street.
Detail of the restaurant Jin Gui.

Tortue

The Tortue Hamburg opened in June 2018 in the central Stadthöfe district. A surface of 8,500 square meters offers a total of 126 rooms. A boutique hotel in the heart of Hamburg – modern, comfortable and unique. It has an international flair – a cozy and modern lifestyle with an urban vibe. With its Asia restaurant, a brasserie and several bars, it offers a new hotspot for guests from all over the world and above all for local people. The project was developed by the Real Estate company Quantum, which brought three gastronomy pros on board: Anne-Marie Bauer as hotel director, Marc Ciunis and Carsten von der Heide as managing directors. The room interior design was created by Kate Hume from Amsterdam. The Hong Kong-based interior designer Joyce Wang is responsible for the design of the Jin Gui restaurant, while

Stephen Williams Associates from Hamburg designed the historical areas in cooperation with David Chipperfiled Architects as well as the Bar Noir and Bar Privée.

The hotel owes its name Tortue Hamburg (French "turtle") to well-dressed dandies in Napoleonic times. As a sign of pure luxury, namely to have time, the gentlemen strolled along the Hamburg boulevards with turtles on lead. And that's what the guest at Tortue Hamburg is invited to celebrate: Time to sharpen the senses for the essentials and the details, to dive into life and discover new horizons. Time to relax and soak up the moment.

Interior view. Bathroom of a suite. Bedroom.
The elegant Bar Blue. Floor plan.

GETTING AROUND. THE TORTUE HAMBURG OFFERS A UNIQUE OVERALL CONCEPT OF GASTRONOMY, HOTELS, EVENTS AND NIGHTLIFE AT ITS HISTORIC LOCATION IN THE HAMBURG STADTHÖFE COURTYARDS. GUESTS EXPERIENCE THE TORTUE HAMBURG AS A SPACE FOR DECELERATED PLEASURES. THE BEST WAY TO EXPLORE IT IS AT THE LUXURIOUS PACE OF A TURTLE (FRENCH: "TORTUE"). "THE TORTUE HAMBURG IS A SPECIAL PLACE THAT MAKES IT EASY FOR GUESTS TO FALL OUT OF TIME". THOSE WHO STILL WANT TO LEAVE THE HOUSE ARE IN THE HEART OF THE CITY, JUST 15 MINUTES AWAY FROM THE ALSTER RIVER, THE SPEICHERSTADT (HARBOR DISTRICT), THE ELBE RIVER, PLANTEN AND BLOMEN PARK.

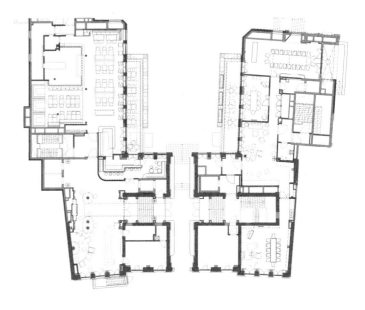

INFORMATION. ARCHITECT>
GREGOR HERBERHOLZ // 2014.
HOLIDAY HOME> 40 SQM //
4 GUESTS // 2 BEDROOMS // 1
BATHROOM. ADDRESS> FELDWEG 29,
BALTIC RESORT AHRENSHOOP,
MECKLENBURG-WESTERN
POMERANIA.
WWW.URLAUBSARCHITEKTUR.DE/
DE/HAUS-MEERSINN

Exterior terrace. Bathroom. Kitchen and dining area.
North elevation from the garden.

Haus Meersinn

AHRENSHOOP,
MECKLENBURG-WESTERN
POMERANIA

The house is situated in the center of Ahrenshoop in a small holiday home settlement. The Baltic beach and the Bodden bay are only a few minutes' walk away. In the surroundings there are also numerous galleries, the Neue Kunsthaus and the Ahrenshoop art museum.

The clearly structured building is clad with battens made of untreated larch wood. Huge wooden windows flood the rooms with light. A ground-deep window to the terrace creates a connection between the living room and the exterior. The large bench on the south side of the living room invites to linger at any time of the year, creating visual contact with the surrounding meadow landscapes and making nature tangible in the house. The size of the two bedrooms was kept to a minimum in order to create the living area as spacious as possible on only 40 square meters of surface. In addition, the bathroom and kitchen were placed in a functional and creative compact "supply core" in the heart of the house. The use of natural materials was a priority for the entire building. All floors are covered with rough slate. The built-in furniture is made of solid oak wood.

Corridor. Front view. Detail of the window bench seat. Interior view of the kitchen. Floor plan.

GETTING AROUND. AHRENSHOOP OFFERS AT ANY TIME OF THE YEAR A WIDE RANGE OF LEISURE ACTIVITIES FOR BOTH NATURE LOVERS AND THOSE INTERESTED IN CULTURE. THE BALTIC SEA BEACH IS ONLY A FEW STEPS AWAY. ALSO THE AHRENSHOOP ART MUSEUM AND A NUMBER OF GALLERIES ARE WITHIN A FEW MINUTES WALKING DISTANCE. THE VORPOMMERSCHE BODDEN-LANDSCHAFT NATIONAL PARK AND ITS IMPRESSIVE COASTAL WOODS AND UNTOUCHED SANDY BEACHES ARE JUST A SHORT BICYCLE RIDE AWAY. IT ONLY TAKES AN ONE HOUR DRIVE BY CAR TO REACH THE HANSEATIC CITY OF STRALSUND WITH ITS GOTHIC BRICK BUILDINGS, WHICH BELONG TO THE UNESCO WORLD HERITAGE, OR VISIT THE OCEAN MUSEUM OZEANEUM.

INFORMATION. ARCHITECTS> KLM-ARCHITEKTEN LEIPZIG GMBH // 2017. 26 LODGES> FROM 48 TO 200 SQM PER LODGE // "KLEINE PERLE" 2 GUESTS, "GROSSES GLÜCK" 4 + 4 GUESTS, "HOCH HINAUS" 6 + 4 GUESTS // 1 TO 3 BEDROOMS // 1 TO 3 BATHROOMS + 1 WC. ADDRESS> SCHWENNAUSTRASSE 37, GLÜCKSBURG, SCHLESWIG-HOLSTEIN. WWW.GLUECK-IN-SICHT.DE

Living area, kitchen, terrace and exterior of the lodge "Großes Glück".

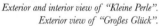

Exterior and interior view of "Kleine Perle".
Exterior view of "Großes Glück".

Glück in Sicht
Ostseelodges

GLÜCKSBURG, SCHLESWIG-HOLSTEIN

The uniqueness of this resort on the fjord of Flensburg is determined by the interaction between interior and nature. Holiday homes of different sizes are placed with care to open up wide views of the coastal and forest landscape. Nordic understatement and elegant simplicity characterize every lodge, from architecture to furnishings. The dark façade, which forms a protective shell, contrasts with the light-flooded, bright interiors. Wood, natural fabrics and soft shades create associations with the beach, dunes and coast.

The heart of the houses is a mixed living and dining area with an open kitchen and large dining table, which offers plenty of space for convivial get-togethers. The sauna, electric fireplace and multimedia equipment make the lodge a cozy place even on colder days. The bedrooms are located in the rear part of the accommodation and offer an ideal retreat. Interior and exterior rooms are connected by the open construction, keeping the view always in the spotlight. The generous windows facing the terraces open up views over the water, forest and meadows as well as the Danish coast.

Lodge "Hoch Hinaus" with sea view.
Terrace "Kleine Perle".

Family bedroom and apartment of the lodge "Hoch Hinaus". Floating terrace of the lodge "Großes Glück". Floor plans.

GETTING AROUND. GLÜCKSBURG ITSELF HAS A NUMBER OF ATTRACTIVE DESTINATIONS TO DISCOVER, INCLUDING THE BEAUTIFUL WATER CASTLE, THE FÖRDELAND THERMAL BATH, THE PLANETARIUM, ROSARIUM AND SALT TEMPLE. NATURE LOVERS CAN EXPLORE THE FLENSBURG FJORD AND ITS BEACHES VIA CYCLE PATHS AND HIKING TRAILS. THE BEAUTIFUL SEAPORT OF FLENSBURG IS LOCATED VERY CLOSE TO GLÜCKSBURG AND INVITES TO TAKE A WALK DOWN ITS ROTE STRASSE AND LITTLE BARS. FOR DANISH DESIGN LOVERS THE CITY OF SØNDERBURG IS A MUST. IT CAN BE REACHED BY FERRY FROM LANGBALLIGAU.

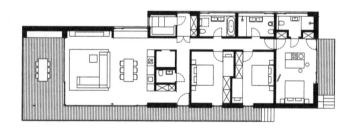

INFORMATION. ARCHITECT>
NOMADS BERLIN // 2017.
APARTMENTS> 400 SQM // 10 GUESTS
// 4 BEDROOM // 4 BATHROOM.
ADDRESS> BERNAUERSTRASSE 25,
BERLIN, GERMANY.
WWW.NOMADSAPT.COM

Interior view of a bedroom. The kitchen.
Ensuite bathroom. Dining and living area.

NOMADS
Apartments

BERLIN

"Even the freest bird needs a nest. We are four of berlins best. Designed for the modern nomads."

The Nomads Apartments offers four apartments that differ in style & subject and can be booked seperately. As a relaxing retreat, a playful creativity factory, a place of stimulating communication and culinary delights, the Nomads Apartments offer provide plenty of options for individual needs. Each of these unique serviced apartments features a different world. Vivid colors, warm materials and luxurious highlights characterize the atmosphere of the Sober, the apartment with 109 square meters for up to 4 persons that includes its own dance floor. The Sober adapts to the moods of its guests. The kitchen becomes a bar, the bed becomes a dance floor.

The Apartment Flow with its East Asian details presents itself as an urban retreat and quiet oasis with a size of 147 square meters and space for up to 6 people. The open kitchen is equipped with a teppanyaki grill and a long dining table for animated evenings with friends. Pink and gold shades set the tone of the subtle but powerful ambience of the apartment Pretty. The accommodation with garden view and a size of 55 square meters offers space for up to 2 persons. The Nomads Gallery is a minimalistically designed, open space over 2 levels with a size of 80 square meters, which can be used as an exhibition room, work space or pop-up shop.

Kitchen and dining area.
Bedroom with bunk bed.

Kitchen with bar. A bedroom.
The Nomads Gallery.

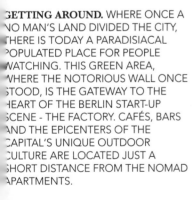

GETTING AROUND. WHERE ONCE A NO MAN'S LAND DIVIDED THE CITY, THERE IS TODAY A PARADISIACAL POPULATED PLACE FOR PEOPLE WATCHING. THIS GREEN AREA, WHERE THE NOTORIOUS WALL ONCE STOOD, IS THE GATEWAY TO THE HEART OF THE BERLIN START-UP SCENE - THE FACTORY. CAFÉS, BARS AND THE EPICENTERS OF THE CAPITAL'S UNIQUE OUTDOOR CULTURE ARE LOCATED JUST A SHORT DISTANCE FROM THE NOMAD APARTMENTS.

INFORMATION. ARCHITECTS>
FERDINAND VON HOHENZOLLERN //
2003 AND 2014. 1 HOLIDAY HOME
(OLD) AND 2 HOLIDAY HOMES WITH
TWO APARTMENTS EACH (NEW)>
406 SQM AND 167 SQM // 9 AND 16
GUESTS // 5 AND 8 BEDROOMS //
3 AND 6 BATHROOMS.
ADDRESS> ORT FERGITZ 1-4,
GERSWALDE, BRANDENBURG.
WWW.GUT-FERGITZ.DE

Gut Fergitz am See

GERSWALDE, BRANDENBURG

Gut Fergitz north of Berlin in the Uckermark, only an hour's drive away. On the shore of Lake Oberuckersee, the former agricultural property has been converted into a holiday home. The complex consists of several barns made of field stone, and modern cubes have been inserted between them. There are two holiday flats in each of the two houses built in a modern style. Large panorama windows and the extensive terraces frame the wide view on the lake, the fields and the terminal moraine landscape with hills. Sand-colored walls, ceilings and floors with anhydride screed look discreet in the context of the great variety of views through the large windows, but a mixture of modern and old furniture brings them to life. On cooler days guests may relax by the fireplace. The architectural language consciously contrasts with any rural romanticism and bridges the gap to the local architecture with materials such as plaster, old bricks and wood. When renovating the fieldstone house attached to the mighty barn, contemporary space concepts were combined with the rustic charm of wooden beams. Gut Fergitz also is a place devoted to art. During the biennial UM festival for contemporary art, music and literature, art installations are shown on the estate grounds and concerts and readings take place in the barn.

View from the terrace. Living room with fireplace. Exterior view. View from the garden.

Terrace. View of the stone house. Surroundings.
Floor plans. Interior view of the kitchen.

GETTING AROUND. THE CHARMING UCKERMARK WITH ITS HILLS, LAKES AND FORESTS HAS DEVELOPED INTO ONE OF THE MOST POPULAR LOCAL LEISURE SPOTS FOR CREATIVE BERLINERS. THE KARL FLAT BATHING AREA IS ONLY A FEW HUNDRED METERS AWAY FROM FERGITZ, WHERE PEOPLE CAN HAVE A SWIM, CANOE, SURF OR FISH. THE BERLIN-USEDOM CYCLING PATH RUNS ALONG THE EASTERN SHORE OF THE LAKE. THE PARK DER GROSSE GARTEN IN GERSWALDE IS ONLY 12 KM AWAY AND INVITES PEOPLE TO LINGER AND RELISH THE MOMENT. BOITZENBURG CASTLE IS ABOUT 30 KM AWAY.

INFORMATION. ARCHITECT>
MARTIN FOCKS // 1999. 7 HOLIDAY
APARTMENTS> 20 UP TO 100 SQM
EACH APARTMENT // 28 GUESTS //
9 BEDROOMS // 9 BATHROOMS.
ADDRESS> DORFSTR. 30, LODDIN,
MECKLENBURG-WESTERN
POMERANIA.
WWW.FOCKS-FERIEN.DE
WWW.ALTE-SCHEUNE-LODDIN.DE

Open kitchen and dining area.
Interior view. Living room. View from
the garden. Side view.

Alte Scheune

LODDIN,
MECKLENBURG-WESTERN
POMERANIA

The seven holiday apartments full of character are part of a listed building which is located on the beautiful island of Usedom. Guests can enjoy the peace and silence of the surroundings and relax from everyday life. The use of ecological building materials was a major priority during the conversion, so it was possible to preserve the monument in its original state and still meet today's standards of quality living.

Apartments ranging in size from 20 to 100 square metres were created after the original division of the old barn of Loddin. Each of the seven apartments has its own terrace and thus a direct connection to the surrounding nature.

A 2,000 square metre meadow, directly on the reed belt, attracts with wide views and leaves enough space to relax or romp around with kids. There is also access to the Achterwasser (backwater) for bathing.

View to the bedroom. Living room. Surroundings. Terrace view.

GETTING AROUND. LODDIN - A SMALL PICTURESQUE PLACE AT A NARROW POINT OF THE ISLAND OF USEDOM. THE PLACE IS SITUATED AT A HEADLAND THAT LEADS TO THE ACHTERWASSER, THE WATERS ENCLOSED BY THE USEDOM ISLAND AND THE MAINLAND. THIS PARTICU-LARITY, HAVING THE ACHTERWASSER ON ONE SIDE AND THE OPEN BALTIC SEA ON THE OTHER, MAKES LODDIN SOMETHING VERY SPECIAL ON USEDOM. LODDINER HÖFT, THE NATURE RESERVE SOUTH OF LODDIN, EXTENDS FAR TO THE ACHTER-WASSER. THE STEEP COAST ABOVE THE WESTERN SHORE OFFERS A GREAT PANORAMIC VIEW OF THE PENINSULAS OF GNITZ AND LIEPER WINKEL AS WELL AS THE MAINLAND COAST OF POMERANIA.

INFORMATION. ARCHITECTS>
STUDIO LOT VERONIKA KAMMERER,
FORMAT ELF STEFAN HANNINGER //
2005/2013. THEME HOUSES, DESIGN
AND BOUTIQUE HOTEL> 30,000 SQM //
26 GUESTS // 1 BEDROOM PER THEME
HOUSE, 2 BEDROOMS PER COTTAGE //
1 BATHROOM PER HOUSE. ADDRESS>
BRUNNDOBL 16, BAD BIRNBACH,
BAVARIA.
WWW.HOFGUT.INFO

*Relaxation area with large window. Dining and
living area. View of the terrace with fireplace.*

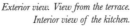
Exterior view. View from the terrace.
Interior view of the kitchen.

Hofgut
Hafnerleiten

BAD BIRNBACH, BAVARIA

A few kilometers from the Lower Bavarian town of Bad Birnbach, in the midst of nature, you will find the Hafnerleiten manor with its 15 very original accommodations. The seven themed and three little holiday homes as well as two suites at the pond and the three new single rooms are each unique and lovingly furnished. The theme houses have been designed, each with a unique floor plan by Studio Lot. Format Elf created the three Rottaler Longhouses in 2013, by the lake, field and forest, which offer even more space and privacy. Their size makes them ideal for longer stays. They come with a fully equipped kitchen, outdoor fireplace and several terraces. The infrared cabins, cozy bunks with an excellent view of the starry sky and bathtubs with a panoramic view of the countryside guarantee a pleasant atmosphere

regardless of the weather. In 1999, Erwin Rückerl and his wife Anja Horn-Rückerl opened Lower Bavaria's first cooking school. Culinary delights play an essential role at the Hofgut. The owners offer cooking or barista courses and the evening menus at the family table provide a cosy and relaxing atmosphere, raising the spirits of the heart. A walk in the countryside, the cooking school or the house library, in addition to the spa cubes, offer a carefree retreat and a short break from "being online". The guests enjoy the time without Internet, television or mobile phone in their rooms, suites and theme houses, allowing them to relax and recharge their batteries. But of course no one has to manage without Wi-Fi, which is available free of charge in the main building.

Side view from the garden. Bedroom.
Detail of a window. Bathroom with abat-jour.

GETTING AROUND. NATURE IS THE PERFECT PLACE TO ENJOY A BREAK AND REST. IF YOU ARE LOOKING FOR SOME ENTERTAINMENT, THE NEXT GOLF COURSE IS JUST 5 KM AWAY AND IS ONE OF THE LARGEST GOLF RESORTS IN EUROPE. THERE ARE ALSO FOUR POPULAR SPAS IN THE IMMEDIATE VICINITY, IN BAD GRIESBACH, BAD FÜSSING AND GEINBERG IN AUSTRIA. THE THREE-RIVER CITY OF PASSAU WITH ITS CATHEDRAL, FORTRESS AND HISTORIC CITY CENTER IS 40 KM AWAY.

INFORMATION. ARCHITECTS> THE CONVERSION WAS CARRIED OUT ON THEIR OWN INITIATIVE - NO ARCHITECT WAS COMMISSIONED // 2017. BED&BREAKFAST > 50 SQM // 10 GUESTS // 3 BEDROOMS // 3 BATHROOMS. ADDRESS> MEMMINGERSTRASSE 14, KRONBURG-ILLERBEUREN, BAVARIA. WWW.KAMMER.REST

View from the garden. Interior view
Living room. Bedroom. Exterior view.

d'Kammer

KRONBURG-ILLERBEUREN, BAVARIA

"What to do with grandma Anna's farmhouse?" That's the question Julia and Michael asked themselves. It is an old farmhouse in the middle of a village in the beautiful Allgäu region. It is the house of their family. Already for many generations. With a story that shouldn't stop... that's why they transformed the farmhouse of their grandma Anna into a Bed & Breakfast - d'Kammer - a B&B in which the guest can experience the charm of grandma's farmhouse. The sound of the creaking wooden floors directs the thoughts to a time when there was no TV and no Facebook. With a mixture of old and new, you will find an accommodation that is stylish - modern - casual. The couple runs its guesthouses with love and passion and also values high-quality products from the region. They live the spirit of slow food and not only offer cheese from their girlfriend's

cheese shop, they also tell guests who baked the rolls and where the chickens live that laid the egg. Julia and Michael, together with Anna, Oskar and Selma, that's the young family who shake up the beds for the guests and create a delicious breakfast for them..."And so come and fill Grandma's house with life!" City, country, river instead of Ipad and television (which consciously does not exist here). And in front of the house there is a small playground with a railway and a racing stable for the little ones. The big ones can lounge in the garden, squint in the sun on the bench in front of the house or watch the village life from the new roof terrace. Authentic placid Allgäu.

Dining room. View of the garden. Outdoor area.
Playground. Floor plans.

GETTING AROUND. EXCURSIONS:
THE FARM MUSEUM CAN BE REACHED
IN ONLY 5 MINUTES WALKING
DISTANCE. WITH ALL ITS ACTIVITIES
LIKE ROLLING AROUND IN THE HAY
AND BOWLING ON AN OLD
OUTDOOR BOWLING ALLEY,
CANOEING OR SWIMMING ON THE
RIVER ILLER. THE BEACH IS ONLY 5
MINUTES AWAY. THE SKYWALKTREE-
TOP- PATH, THE RAVENSBURGER
MUSEUM (GAMES) AND THE
PLAYGROUND ARE CLOSE BY. CULTURE:
THE CITIES OF MEMMINGEN,
KEMPTEN AND ULM ARE ALL WITHIN
EASY REACH. THE KRONBURG CASTLE
INVITES TO CONCERTS RIGHT NEXT
DOOR. OTHER ACTIVITIES: SWIMMING
IN THE MOST BEAUTIFUL LAKES,
HIKING AFTER A 45 MINUTE TRIP TO
THE MOUNTAINS OR IN 30 MINUTES
TO LAKE CONSTANCE.

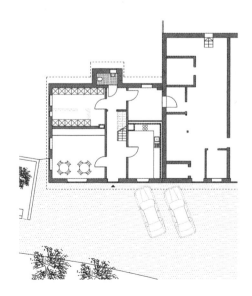

Exterior view from the front.
Dining room. Living room.

INFORMATION. ARCHITECTS> KIRSTEN AND TOBIAS FELLER, PETER MERL // 2017. HOTEL> 960 SQM // 26 GUESTS // 12 BEDROOMS // 12 BATHROOMS. ADDRESS> AN DER TRIFT 19, CLAUSTHAL-ZELLERFELD, LOWER SAXONY. WWW.DIEFELLEREI.DE

Die Fellerei

CLAUSTHAL-ZELLERFELD,
LOWER SAXONY

The Fellerei is a former brewery in the upper Harz mountains, which was for many years a guest house and later gradually converted into a hotel. In 2016 Kirsten and Tobias Feller took over the house and lovingly renovated it. With a love for detail, the owners decorated each of the twelve rooms with pieces of furnishings they had collected. Nordic design, vintage and a touch of color are the basic ingredients of this "Harz mix" style.

Each room has its unique character just like the house itself. Between old and new, first and second hand, restored and left in their natural state, playful and unconventional, rich on ideas and handmade. Rooms with soul, as house and courtyard set the tone. The Fellerei is a wild piece of improvisation in architectural terms, living over the years with constant modifications, always in motion and never completely done. Thus it may happen that something is different at the next visit. Since sustainability is an important focus, a lot of things are actually still in use, even though they are no longer modern or new. This creates a lively place to relax and to be - either alone or in the company of other guests. A house with quiet corners inside, in the courtyard and in the garden and with creative dishes from regional cuisine, seasoned with love and passion. The meals are served in cozy dining rooms on small and large tables.

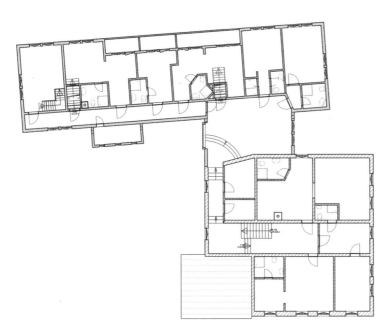

GETTING AROUND. TO FEEL LIKE AT HOME AND ON HOLIDAY IS THE SPIRIT OF HOSPITALITY OF THE FELLEREI. TO GET SPOILED AND SET OFF TO EXPLORE THE HARZ. THIS IS THE PERFECT DEPARTURE POINT FOR HIKING, IN SUMMER OR WINTER, WITH OR WITHOUT SNOWSHOES, CROSS-COUNTRY SKIING, CLIMBING AND RUNNING, CYCLING AND SWIMMING IN THE LAKE. THE SMALL, BUT FINE HARZ-SPA AT THE FELLEREI OFFERS YOGA, MASSAGE AND SAUNA. SIMPLE AND REDUCED TO THE ESSENTIAL. AFTER A HIKE OR BIKE TOUR, GUESTS MAY SIMPLY ENJOY PEACE AND RELAXATION OR JUST DO NOTHING.

Bedroom with green walls.
Floor plan. Interior view.

A bedroom. View of the courtyard from
the top. Interior view of the dining area.

INFORMATION. ARCHITECTS>
ARCHITEKTURSTUDIO SCHROTH //
2018. HYBRID HOTEL> 340 SQM //
24 GUESTS // 11 BEDROOMS //
11 BATHROOMS. ADDRESS> VORM
WÜRZBURGER TOR 15, ROTHENBURG
OB DER TAUBER, BAVARIA.
WWW.MITTERMEIERSALTEREGO.DE

Bedroom. View through the corridor.
Entrance area with dining table.

Dining and kitchen area.
Front view from the garden.

Mittermeiers Alter Ego

ROTHENBURG OB DER TAUBER,
BAVARIA

In front of the gateways of the historical centre of Rothenburg, a former entrepreneur mansion from the Gründerzeit, the Wilhelminian era, was converted into a hotel. The result is an individual and charming guesthouse with the quality of a high-end hotel and the relaxed atmosphere of a private apartment. The architectural concept interprets the old building structure in a completely new way and sets history and modernity in harmony.

The eleven open-plan hotel rooms were equipped with a 3-D Mondrian, which also serves as a room divider, shelf, wardrobe, room lighting, seating and bathroom boundary. With their effect of closeness and distance, the elements create a spatial diversity that is both generous and transparent. Guests have access to an honesty bar, a kitchen for self-catering and to the neighboring restaurant.

Its black exterior gives the building a sensual look and the monochrome colors interact with light and shadow creating an expressive effect. Shell limestone walls clearly pop out of the black façade and reflect the ancient art of natural stone craftsmanship. Like dancing figures, the walls move over the façade of the hotel, creating a new lightness.

Interior view of the bathroom. Bedroom with bathtub.
Staircase. Floor plans.

GETTING AROUND. EXPLORE THE OLD TOWN OF ROTHENBURG. THE TOP 10 SIGHTS ARE RIGHT IN FRONT OF THE HOTEL: THE MARKET SQUARE WITH THE CITY HALL, THE PLÖNLEIN, THE CITY WALL WITH ITS TOWERS, THE CASTLE GARDEN, THE CRIME MUSEUM, THE CHRISTMAS VILLAGE, THE JAKOBSKIRCHE CHURCH, THE HISTORIENGEWÖLBE AND THE DOUBLE BRIDGE AT THE TAUBER VALLEY. ACCOMPANY THE NIGHT GUARD OF ROTHENBURG ON HIS EVENING ROUND, DISCOVER MEDIEVAL CURIOSITIES IN THE CRIME MUSEUM AND THE HIGHLIGHTS OF THE HISTORY OF ROTHENBURG HOSTED IN THE REICHSSTADT-MUSEUM.

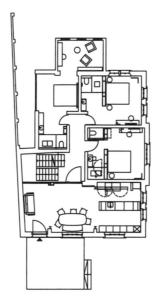

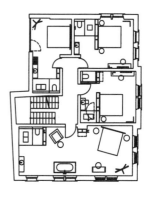

INFORMATION. ARCHITECTS> DIRK MICHEL. ARCHITEKT BDA // 2016. HOTEL> 1,360 SQM // 129 GUESTS // 59 BEDROOMS // 61 BATHROOMS. ADDRESS> GURLITTSTRASSE 23, HAMBURG. WWW.HOTELWEDINA.DE

A bedroom with blue walls. Detail of a bedroom and bathroom. Interior view.

Hotel Wedina Rotes Haus

HAMBURG

The Wedina, the main house and its three sister houses are located in Gurlittstrasse in the middle of the Hamburg district St.Georg. In addition to the reception, the Rotest Haus also houses the breakfast room and lobby on the ground floor, as well as 21 hotel rooms on the 3 upper floors.

In 2016, within the framework of a core renovation, these were newly conceived and redesigned. Natural materials determine the aesthetics of the rooms. Oiled, solid oak floors and mineral colors on walls and ceilings provide a cozy warmth. The bathrooms are mainly characterized by shell limestone (natural stone) in combination with mineral splinter in the showers.
The color of the walls comes from the Le Corbusier color palette, the furniture is made of oak like the floor.

All hotel rooms got their own color. There are no darkening curtains in the rooms on purpose. External electrical screens, which are automatically raised or lowered when entering or leaving the room, provide sun protection. The room is darkened by folding shutters inside the window reveals.

The Wedina is a hotel Garni, which offers a very good breakfast, and guests can also enjoy it in the hotel garden in summer. The hotel is committed to literature; well-known authors give readings and leave their signed works in the hotel, filling the Wedinas library over the years.

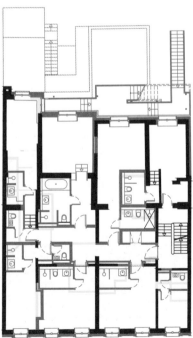

GETTING AROUND. THE WEDINA IS LOCATED BETWEEN THE AUSSENALSTER AND THE LANGE REIHE, THE HEART OF THAT PART OF THE TOWN. THE JETTIES OF THE AUSSENALSTER ARE SITUATED CLOSE BY AND INVITE PEOPLE TO STAY FOR A WHILE. THE CONNECTION TO THE CENTRAL RAILWAY STATION IS VERY GOOD. IT CAN ALSO BE EASILY REACHED BY FOOT. SOME OF THE MOST FAMOUS MUSEUMS OF THE CITY, SUCH AS THE HAMBURGER KUNST-HALLE OR THE MUSEUM FÜR KUNST UND GEWERBE ARE LOCATED RIGHT NEXT TO THE CENTRAL STATION. THE DEUTSCHE SCHAUSPIELHAUS IS A GREAT PLACE TO VISIT FOR THEATRE LOVERS. THE DISTRICT LIVES FROM A WIDE VARIETY OF CULTURAL INFLUENCES. THE LANGE REIHE IS KNOWN FOR ITS RICH CAFÉ, RESTAURANT AND BAR SCENE.

Bedroom with green walls.
Floor plan. Exterior view.

A Bedroom. View on the folding
wooden shutters. Bathroom.

INFORMATION. ARCHITECTS>
OXEN ARCHITEKTEN // 2016.
HOTEL> 336 SQM // 13 GUESTS //
7 BEDROOMS // 7 BATHROOMS.
ADDRESS> GUTSVERWALTUNG HAUS
AUEL, LOHMAR , NORTH RHINE-
WESTPHALIA.
WWW.SCHLOSSAUEL.DE/INDEX.PHP/
LAYOUT-OPTIONS/GOLF-LODGE

Interior view. Exterior view.
A bedroom. Street view by night.

Golf Lodge
Schloss Auel

LOHMAR, NORTH RHINE-WESTPHALIA

The Golf Lodge was erected on the site of a demolished revenue office on the castle grounds as a supplement to the existing hotel complex. Priority of the design is to provide a contemporary answer to the task of integration into the existing ensemble – from new to old.

This aesthetic question is answered stylistically by the use of a contemporary formal language and modern materials. The building itself is clearly defined as a prototype of a gabled roof house. The roof and wall are covered with slate in dynamic double layers, the gable sides are clad in wood and painted red, like the respective parts of the castle and its annexes.

The entire complex is built in solid wood. Walls, ceilings and roof soffits get their uniqueness from precious wood surfaces made of Black Forest silver fir. They characterize the entire interior design together with other natural materials. The light-colored, unobtrusive wood structure is an attractive contrast to the black, mineral building shell and the wet cell, which is made of polished slate.

View from the garden.
Bathroom.

Living area. Details of the front.
Sleeping area. Floor plans.

GETTING AROUND. THE GOLF
LODGE IS LOCATED IN BERGISCHES
LAND, IN A LISTED ENSEMBLE OF THE
FORMER CASTLE AUEL, IN THE HEART
OF A SEVERAL HA LARGE AREA
OF THE CASTLE AND GOLF AREA IN
AGGERTAL. THE SURROUNDINGS ARE
VAST NATURAL LANDSCAPES, WHICH
ARE PERFECT FOR HIKING AND
CYCLING. TYPICAL TO THE REGION
ARE THE MANY RIVERS AND LAKES,
THE REGIONAL CUISINE WITH THE
BERGISCHE KAFFEETAFEL AND THE
HALF-TIMBERED AND SLATE HOUSES
LOCATED IN THE NUMEROUS AND
CLOSE HISTORICAL TOWN CENTERS.

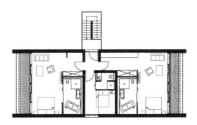

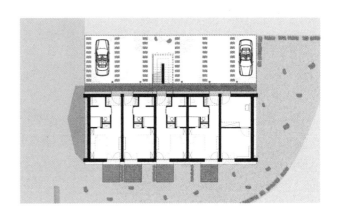

INFORMATION. ARCHITECTS>
ANDREAS BRAND AND JONAS
LÄNGENFELDER // 2017.
GUESTHOUSE> 120 SQM // 8 GUESTS //
4 BEDROOMS // 2 BATHROOMS.
ADDRESS> GRIMMSTRASSE 3,
MUNICH, BAVARIA.
WWW.VIERZIMMERHOTEL.COM

*Kitchen. Interior view. A bedroom seperated
from the living room by a white "in-walls-plants"
textile structure.*

A bedroom. Detail of the custommade furniture.

Vier Zimmer

MUNICH, BAVARIA

Vier Zimmer is a small, exceptional boutique guesthouse in the Isarvorstadt, a beautiful district of Munich, with just four rooms. The guest house is part of a listed and renovated town house with beautiful restyled rooms.

"Be our guests and use a fully equipped common kitchen, grab a beer or a lemonade from the fridge and enjoy the green terrace in the courtyard. And take our bikes for free to explore Munich in the easiest way. Perfect for groups and famlies you also can rent two, three or all four rooms as one big apartment for up to 8 people and enjoy the place all by yourself." This, the owners' invitation is the best description of the concept and cordiality of the house.

When the house was purchased in 2017 and got a new coat of paint, the preservation of the original and individual character was of great importance for the further work. The owners developed the extraordinary concept of new, fresh architecture and individual design together with the junior architects of Lineloni Architecture Design from the Innsbruck architecture and culture collective Krater Fajan. The result was a mixture of old and new design classics, modern lighting concepts and unique and individually manufactured furniture. The authentic and special look creates a real feel-good atmosphere.

A bedroom. View of the corridor.

Front at the garden with benches.
Bathroom. Floor plan.

GETTING AROUND. THE VIER ZIMMER IS LOCATED IN A VERY QUIET DOWNTOWN AREA BETWEEN WONDERFUL OLD TOWN HOUSES AT THE FEET OF THE BAVARIA. WHEN THIS STATUE IS ILLUMINATED AT NIGHT AND AS NO OTHER MONUMENT REMINDS OF BAVARIA'S GLORIOUS PAST, ALL GUESTS AND RESIDENTS OF MUNICH ARE FASCINATED BY IT. THE OLD TOWN AROUND THE MARIENPLATZ, THE ENGLISH GARDEN AND THE MAIN STATION ARE 5 MINUTES AWAY BY SUBWAY. THE RIVER ISAR, MUNICH'S LIFELINE, CAN BE REACHED IN 10 MINUTES WALKING DISTANCE. SURROUNDED BY BARS, RESTAURANTS AND BOUTIQUES, THE INHABITANTS ARE FAR AWAY FROM TOURIST CROWDS.

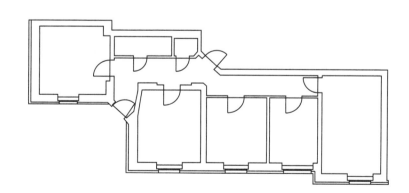

INFORMATION. ARCHITECTS>
ELISOPHIE EULENBURG // 2017.
HOLIDAY HOME> 200 SQM OF LIVING
SPACE // 10 GUESTS // 6 BEDROOMS //
2 BATHROOMS. ADDRESS>
ZEHDENICK, BRANDENBURG.
WWW.DAS-BLAUE-PFERD.DE

Dining and living room.
View throught the corridor.

Das Blaue Pferd

ZEHDENICK, BRANDENBURG

A farmyard with buildings on four sides in the Rupinersee region, for holidays, conferences and cultural retreats. The listed farm is situated one hour north of Berlin in a quiet village on the edge of the Schorfheide biosphere reserve. There is plenty of space and peace to relax and explore the beautiful landscapes of northern Brandenburg or to concentrate on work. The four sourrounding buildings make it a sheltered place, like a small village square or monastery courtyard.

The 200 square metre barn offers space for rehearsals, workshops, desks in the green, making music, studios, readings, film sets, table tennis matches, exhibitions, cinema or theatre. Around the farm there are fruit trees, multicolored flowers, vegetables, herbs and shrubs. The farmhouse has been renovated carefully, taking sustainability into account and in accordance with the requirements of a listed building. Some things are just as simple as they used to be. All furniture and almost all household items are selected from old stocks, repaired, upcycled or homemade. Sustainability has thus become a central design element in the furnishing of the house, alongside of shape and color. The rooms of the farm are the work of artists and designers, who have created a simple and modern design in a historical ambience, surrounded by nature and tranquillity. The farm is perfect for accommodation of single persons or groups. There are 10 beds available. It is also possible to accommodate other guests on mattresses.

View from the garden.
Bedroom with fireplace.

GETTING AROUND. THE FARM IS LOCATED IN THE MIDDLE OF THE WIDE, SPARSELY POPULATED COUNTRYSIDE OF BRANDENBURG, A LAKES AND FORESTS REGION. THE WOODS OF THE SCHORFHEIDE BIOSPHERE RESERVE, ONE OF THE LARGEST FOREST AREAS IN GERMANY, BEGIN RIGHT BEHIND THE VILLAGE. THE ZEHDENICK CLAY PIT AREA OFFERS COUNTLESS CLEAR LAKES FOR SWIMMING RIGHT NEXT DOOR. IN THE NORTH, FOREST PATHS AND LITTLE ROADS TAKE YOU TO THE HILLY LANDSCAPE OF THE UCKERMARK. A TRIP TO THE WEST COULD BE A SHORT STAGE ON THE BERLIN-COPENHAGEN CYCLE PATH, ALONG THE HAVEL PAST THE BRICKWORKS PARK MUSEUM, THROUGH HIMMELPFORT AND FÜRSTENBERG TO LAKE STECHLIN.

Living room. Garden view.
Terrace.

Dining room with benches.
A bedroom. Interior view of the barn.

INFORMATION. ARCHITECTS>
THOMAS KRÖGER ARCHITEKTEN //
2012. HOLIDAY HOME> 140 SQM //
10 GUESTS // 5 BEDROOMS // 2
BATHROOMS. ADDRESS> OT PINNOW
26 A, GERSWALDE, BRANDENBURG.
WWW.DASSCHWARZEHAUS.DE

Living room with fireplace. Side view.
View from the garden.

Das schwarze Haus

GERSWALDE, BRANDENBURG

Das Schwarze Haus is located in the middle of the Uckermark region on theedge of Pinnow, a village with around 90 inhabitants. The house stands freely on a property of 5,000 square meters that includes a small kettle hole, a small pond remaining from the terminal moraine time. Pinnow, a former farm with a manor house, is situated north of the Schorfheide, a hilly landscape interspersed with lakes and forests. Three smaller lakes surround the village itself, the largest having two bathing spots.

The unconventional house is captivating because of Thomas Kröger's clear and consistent architecture. The rooms merge with their surroundings and set the scene for great panoramic views. Well-structured floor plans and puristic design create a tidy yet very pleasant atmosphere. On the lower level there is a spacious living room with six-meter-high ceilings, a fireplace and an open kitchen. Two alcoves, separated from the living room by sliding doors, contain two sleeping places for two guests each. The bathroom has an open bathtub of 2 meters length with views over the countryside. Upstairs, there are two bedrooms for two people each with a guest toilet. By adding extra beds, there is place for a total of ten guests. The rear part of the house contains a working space with its own small library.

GETTING AROUND. THE BEST: THERE'S NOTHING TO DO AND JUST TO ENJOY THE VIEW AND THE SCENERY OR THE HOUSE ITSELF. YOU CAN ALSO SWIM IN THE LAKE, WHICHIS ONLY 900 METERS AWAY, OR EXPLORE THE WONDERFUL SURROUNDINGS BY FOOT. RAW BOATS CAN BE RENTED AT LAKE STERNHAGEN (4 KM) IN THE NEARBY NATURE RESERVE THERE ARE PATHS THAT WON PRIZES BECAUSE OF THEIR BEAUTY. THE LAKE OF STERNHAGEN OFFERS A NICE RUNNING GROUND OF 6 KM LENGTH.

View from the garden with snow.
Sleeping area. Bedroom in the attic.

Study with library. Living room.
Sleeeping alcoves and bathtub with garden view.

INFORMATION. ARCHITECTS>
MATTEO THUN & PARTNERS SRL AND
STEIN HEMMES WIRTZ, LANDSCAPER>
HKK LANDSCHAFTSARCHITEKTUR
GMBH // 2013. VINEYARD COTTAGE>
26 SQM PER COTTAGE // 2 GUESTS PER
COTTAGE // 1 BEDROOM PER
COTTAGE // 1 BATHROOM PER
COTTAGE. ADDRESS> KIRCHENWEG 9,
LONGUICH, RHINELAND-PALATINATE.
WWW.LONGEN-SCHLOEDER.DE

Bedroom. Interior view. View of the garden.
Exterior view.

Winery Longen-Schlöder

ONGUICH, RHINELAND-PALATINATE

The Longen family cultivates the slopes of the Moselle valley in harmony with nature and looks back on a long tradition of viticulture. This place is a little paradise: an orchard surrounded by orchards. The more than 6,500-square-metre property allows guests to experience the most authentic way of living. During the development process, it was important to ensure harmony between the existing wine and fruit-growing structures, the village and nature. Italian architect Matteo Thun supported the family throughout the entire planning and construction phase. Stein-Hemmes-Wirtz architects supervised the construction project on site. Landscape architect Johannes Cox, HKK Landschaftsarchitekten from Frankfurt am Main,designed the individual gardens paying great attention to details. The new winegrowers' cottages,

the large restaurant and the new main building express their philosophy. Guests live in small stone houses built from local slate amidst fruit and walnut trees, lime trees and chestnuts. Some of the 20 cottages can be connected to a family cottage and each of them has a small wooden terrace and its own private garden. It is surrounded by raspberry hedges that are edible, thus you can enjoy your own harvest on the terrace. The 26-square-meter slate houses are bright, clear and reduced in design. Lots of wood, lots of white, natural fabrics and raw materials characterize the interior design. The wooden floor joins the interior with the terrace – a large glass door connects the inside and outside.

Evening garden view.
View of the restaurant.

Bedroom with garden view. Interior view. Detail of the front door. Floor plans and vertical section.

GETTING AROUND. THE LOHNGEN-SCHLÖDER ESTATE OFFERS A WIDE VARIETY OF WINES ON ITS OWN VINEYARDS IN THE MOSELLAGEN. THESE INCLUDE FOR EXAMPLE THE LONGUICHER MAXIMINER HERREN-BERG, LONGUICHER HERRENBERG, SCHWEICHER ANNABERG AND MEH-RINGER ZELLERBERG. TRIER AND ALL ITS ROMAN HERITAGE IS APPROX. 15 MINUTES DRIVE BY CAR AWAY. THE ROMANTIC WINE TOWN OF BERNKASTEL-KUES IS JUST AN HALF HOUR DRIVE AWAY AND THE TOWN OF LUXEMBOURG ONLY AROUND 60 KILOMETER. THE MOSELLE VALLEY HAS MANY HIKING AND CYCLING TRAILS TO EXPLORE.

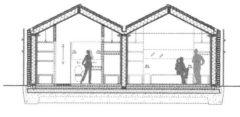

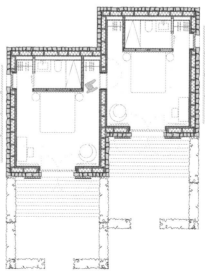

INFORMATION. ARCHITECTS>
A-BASE | BÜRO FÜR ARCHITEKTUR //
2012. APARTMENT AND TEMPORARY
LIVING SPACE> 82 SQM // 4 GUESTS //
2 BEDROOMS // 2 BATHROOMS.
ADDRESS> ALTONAERSTRASSE 10,
BERLIN.
WWW.ROOMBERGS.DE

Rio Marie

BERLIN

The Apartment Rio Marie with its interesting history is located in the middle of Berlin, close to the Tiergarten and the Siegessäule. The old Hansa quarter became the central area of the International Building Exhibition (IBA 57) in 1957 in order to represent the "city of tomorrow". Architects from all over the world were invited to design buildings that still today are role models for modern architecture and urban planning. They built an open city vision in post-war Berlin. Among them was the Brazilian Oscar Niemeyer, who built an 8-storey social housing complex with 78 two to four room apartments in Altonaer Strasse 4-14 at the same time as the buildings for Brasilia, the new capital of Brazil. Now converted into condominiums, the former 4-room apartment was relaunched in 2012. The apartment mutated into an amazingly modern, open-plan apartment with a spacious living and cooking area, two well-proportioned bedrooms with dressing areas and two bathrooms. The design is a tribute to the 50s. Furniture with light, thin materials and flared legs is reminiscent of a time when luxury was still scarce. Linoleum, porcelain stoneware floor tiles, narrow door handles by Johannes Potente in a free interpretation and combination with the contemporary: the apartment arrived in the 20th century after its renovation.

Dinig area with a brazilian Jacaranda wood wall.
View of the kitchen. Exterior view. Working space.

Bedroom. Bathroom. Living room.
Floor plan. Interior view.

GETTING AROUND. THE OSCAR-NIEMEYER-HOUSE IS LOCATED IN THE IMMEDIATE VICINITY OF SCHLOSS BELLEVUE, THE OFFICIAL RESIDENCE OF THE GERMAN FEDERAL PRESIDENT, THE PRESIDENTIAL OFFICE, THE SIEGESSÄULE (VICTORY COLUMN), THE AKADEMIE DER KÜNSTE (ACADEMY OF THE ARTS), THE STRASSE DES 17. JUNI, BERLIN'S MOST IMPORTANT EASTWEST ARTERY. ONE STATION WITH THE S-BAHN TO BERLIN'S NEW CENTRAL STATION, TWO STATIONS TO THE ZOOLOGISCHER GARTEN STATION, AND STILL SURROUNDED BY THE PARK TIERGARTEN, THE GREEN LUNG IN THE HEART OF THE CITY WITH THE MOST CHARMING BEER GARDENS, LAWNS FOR SUNBATHING, RUNING TRACKS. HERE IS A LOOSE MIXTURE OF HIGHRISE AND LOW-RISE BUILDINGS WITH A LOT OF GREENERY AROUND THE CENTRAL HANSAPLATZ. JUST IN FRONT THE SHOPPING MALL, CHURCH, THE CINEMA (NOW GRIPSTHEATER), A LIBRARY AND A KINDERGARTEN.

INFORMATION. ARCHITECT> HEINRICH MARTIN BRUNS ARCHITEKT BDA // 2012. HOLIDAY HOME "EINS" AND "ZWO"> 100 SQM EACH // 6 GUESTS HOUSE "EINS", 5 GUESTS HOUSE "ZWO" // 3 BEDROOMS HOUSE "EINS", 2 BEDROOMS + 1 GUEST BED HOUSE "ZWO"// 2 BATHROOMS HOUSE "EINS", 1 BATHROOM + 1 SHOWER WITH WC HOUSE "ZWO". ADDRESS> KÖHN'S ÜBERGANG 9, WITTDÜN, AMRUM, SCHLESWIG-HOLSTEIN. WWW.DUENENHAUS-AMRUM.DE

Exterior of house "Eins" and "Zwo".
Dining room house "Eins". Living room
house "Eins" from above.

Dünenhaus

AMRUM, SCHLESWIG-HOLSTEIN

The 2-family house planned as a holiday home is located on the beautiful North Frisian island. Due to its location in a nature reserve it was built deeper and divided into two living areas with wind-protected terrace courtyards on the south side. The floor plans were designed as open spaces. Ground floor and top floor are connected by airy spaces and develop into a light-flooded room sculpture.

Each apartment has a surface of approx. 100 square meters, spread over several rooms in the ground floor and attic floor. The architects designed themselves the modern interior and the atmospheric lighting. The house consists of a wooden frame with internal thermal insulation and wooden ceiling.

Wooden and metal windows have triple glazing and narrow, closed air ventilation wings. The house was designed and built as a low-energy house. The floor heating system is gas powered and provides a pleasant temperature. Roof collectors supply hot water.

The property in the dunes is only fixed at the built-up parts and thus does its environment justice. Beach oat and heather are growing everywhere on all unbuilt parcels. The paved areas consist of wood or concrete slabs which have been installed without sealing on the dune sand using a loose gravel fill.

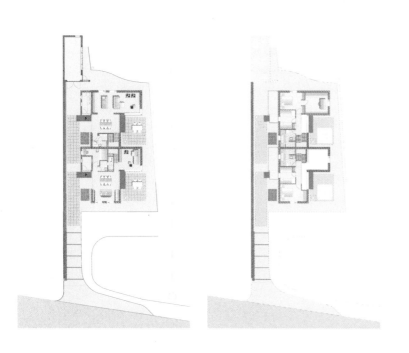

GETTING AROUND. IN CLOSE PROXIMITY TO THE UNIQUE DUNE LANDSCAPE OF THE NORTH SEA ISLAND OF AMRUM LIES THE WOODFRAME HOUSE DÜNENHAUS. THE BEACH WITH AN ADVENTURE PLAYGROUND AND A PROMENADE IS ONLY A FEW METERS AWAY. THE LIGHTHOUSE, THE SEA SIGN HARBOUR ON THE TIDAL FLAT SIDE AND THE VILLAGES OF THE ISLAND CAN BE REACHED BY FOOT OR BICYCLE. FERRY TERMINALS, SHOPPING FACILITIES, CAFÉS AND RESTAURANTS ARE IN THE NEIGHBORHOOD.

View from the western part of the garden.
Floor plans. Foyer house "Eins".

Living room house "Eins".
Dining room house "Zwo".
Living room house "Zwo".

INFORMATION. ARCHITECTS>
CBAG.STUDIO ARCHITEKTEN BDA,
LANDSCAPER> DANE LANDSCHAFTS-
PLANER, INTERIOR DESIGN> NICOLAY
DESIGN, MOBILIAR PUBLIC SPACES>
CONNI KOTTE // 2015. EXPANSION>
CBAG.STUDIO ARCHITEKTEN BDA,
INTERIOR DESIGN> CBAG.STUDIO
ARCHITEKTEN BDA, SUITE OG>
CONNI KOTTE // 2019. HOTEL>
5,800 SQM // 100 GUESTS // 50
BEDROOMS // 50 BATHROOMS.
ADDRESS> PRÄLAT-SUBTIL RING 22,
SAARLOUIS, SAARLAND.
WWW.LAMAISON-HOTEL.DE

La Maison

SAARLOUIS, SAARLAND

The La Maison combines tradition and modernity. Old and new. History and change. Opposites attract each other. A renovated villa, formerly the Higher Administrative Court, finds its counterpart in a minimalist new building in the north. In the south it is flanked by the former caretaker's house. At the back, the trio is bound by a wooded park and that gives the ensemble a new identity.

The house welcomes its guests as a grande dame with a very stylish entrée. The new building is a little more discreet, but nevertheless it displays a changing face. Wrapped in a screen of anodised aluminium folding shutters, its structure begins to live up to the guests' needs. They electrically control the interplay between transparency and protection.

La Maison creates a fascinating tension between classicism and zeitgeist. Between freedom and security, selfconfidence and caution.

Street view. Interior view. Lobby Louis Salon.
Evening view of the new hotel building.

Garden view. Spiral staircase. Detail of the furniture.
Floor plan of the ground level.

GETTING AROUND. SAARLOUIS WAS BUILT BY LOUIS XIV AS A FORTIFIED CITY. ITS HEXAGONAL GROUND PLAN STILL DETERMINES THE INNER TOWN TODAY. IT IS SITUATED NEAR THE FRENCH BORDER AND IS KNOWN FOR ITS FRENCH FLAIR. GUESTS CAN QUICKLY GET TO METZ AND VISIT ITS SIGHTS, MUSEUMS AND ART CENTERS SUCH AS THE CENTER POMPIDOU. VÖLKLINGER HÜTTE IS AN UNESCO WORLD CULTURAL HERITAGE SITE. THE FORMER IRONWORK, KNOWN FORT ITS BIENNIAL URBAN ART FESTIVAL IS CLOSE BY.

Street view by night.
Interior view of the library.

INFORMATION. ARCHITECT>
BERND VORDERMEIER, INTERIOR
DESIGN> HAIDL-MADL // 2013.
BAVARIAN FOREST HOUSE> 56 SQM // 2
GUESTS // 1 BEDROOM // 1 BATHROOM
ADDRESS> MARCHHÄUSER 2,
HAIDMÜHLE, BAVARIA.
WWW.HAIDL-MADL-FERIENWOHNEN.D

*Exterior view. Interior
view of the library.*

Haidl-Madl,
Alte Liebe

HAIDMÜHLE, BAVARIA

The generous, 300-year-old Bavarian forest house has been redefined through careful interventions, discreet quotations and the use of regional woods. It now houses the family living room, a small shop and three holiday apartments. Interventions and dismantling have been limited to the necessary, existing structures have been preserved and integrated into new ones.

The accommodation Alte Liebe offers an extraordinary retreat as the original structure of the house was carefully respected. The disproportionate façade openings were restructured with protrusions and setbacks and aligned to the façade to mirror the landscape.

The use of natural materials, such as white fir, reflects the connection to the Bavarian Forest. Its modern window elements create an excellent contact with nature and ensure guests' desired privacy.

Living room. Blue room.

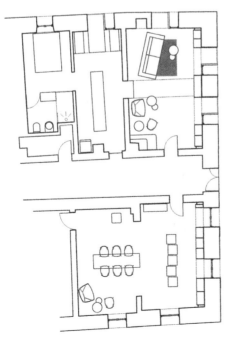

GETTING AROUND. THE HAIDLMADL IS LOCATED IN THE MIDDLE OF AN IDEAL-TYPICAL, CLOSE-TO-NATURE CULTURAL LANDSCAPE ON THE EUROPEAN GREEN BELT. SITUATED IN A CALM SETTING BETWEEN THE BAVARIAN FOREST AND THE SUMAVA NATIONAL PARKS IT IS THE PERFECT DEPARTURE POINT FOR A VARIETY OF LEISURE ACTIVITIES. FOR CULTURE AND NATURE LOVERS AS WELL AS SPORTS ENTHUSIASTS. THE WORLD HERITAGE CITIES OF REGENSBURG AND KRUMAU AS WELL AS THE THREE-RIVER CITY OF PASSAU ARE NOT FAR AWAY AND CAN BE EXPLORED ON A DAY TRIP.

Front view from the garden. Floor plan. Living room.

A bedroom. Kitchen and dining area. View from the garden.

INFORMATION. ARCHITECTS> BAUMRAUM, ANDREAS WENNING // 2019. TREEHOUSE> 54 SQM PER TREEHOUSE + 12 SQM TERRACE // 2–4 GUESTS // 2 BEDROOMS // 1 BATHROOM. ADDRESS> LANDSTRASSE 36, LÜTETSBURG, LOWER SAXONY. WWW.LUETETSBURG-LODGES.DE

Exterior view by night. Bedroom. Living and kitchen area.

Lütetsburg Baumhaus - Lodges

LÜTETSBURG, LOWER SAXONY

The complex consists of three large tree houses on stilts located on the edge of a small forest. It is surrounded by the gently rolling meadows of the golf course, hedges, small groups of trees and the East Frisian landscape with its typical wide views. The tree houses integrate harmoniously the existing tree population and face south with the prominent gable façades. The clear architectural language is a modern interpretation of the archetypal house. The outer shell with the wood cladding of the front made of larch, the windows and the metallic roof covering are accentuated by a dark anthracite tone. Inside, the concept continues and creates a warm atmosphere that matches the surroundings. The idea of creating a branch graphic on the large windows was developed in cooperation with nature conservationists.

First and foremost, the graphics should enable the birds to visually perceive the transparent surfaces and thus prevent the animals from a collision. Each of the tree houses has an open terrace on a lower level and a covered balcony at the gable wall. This is the best place to enjoy the beautiful landscape and to observe wild animals such as fallow deers, hares and several birds. A special experience is the open gallery with the sleeping area on the second level. It offers through its large windows a spectacular view of the treetops and the vast scenery.

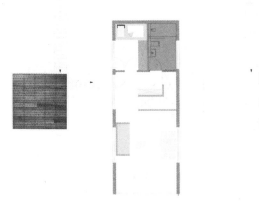

GETTING AROUND. SCHLOSSPARK LÜTETSBURG, THE LARGEST PRIVATE ENGLISH LANDSCAPE PARK IN NORTHERN GERMANY WITH ALMOST 30 HA OF LAND, IS A SPECIAL SIGHT AND PROVIDES ACCESS TO A WIDE RANGE OF EXPERIENCES. NOT ONLY GOLFING, CYCLING, WALKING AND GEOCACHING, BUT ALSO CULTURAL, SEASONAL EVENTS ENRICH A STAY IN LÜTETSBURG: CONCERTS, READINGS AND OTHER EVENTS TAKE PLACE EITHER IN THE KULTURSCHEUNE, THE BARN, OR OPEN-AIR IN THE PARK OF THE CASTLE.

View from garden. Floor plans.
Interior view from the terrace.

Bedroom in the first floor.
Bathroom. Terrace.

INFORMATION. ARCHITECTS>
EVA FESS-HOLLENBACH // 2017.
HOLIDAY HOME> 160 SQM //
8 GUESTS // 5 BEDROOMS //
2 BATHROOMS. ADDRESS>
BLIESENRADER WEG 13, WIECK A.
DARSS, MECKLENBURG-WESTERN
POMERANIA.
WWW.KAPITAENSHAUS-WIECK.DE

*Living space. View to the living room. Interior view of
the dining room. View from the garden.*

Kapitänshaus Wieck

WIECK A. DARSS,
MECKLENBURG-WESTERN
POMERANIA

The Kapitänshaus, a captain's house built around 1850, is located on the peninsual Fischland-Darss-Zingst and has a typical reed roof and a traditional entrance door. Together with the service building it is listed as an individual monument and stands on a 1,600 square meters property with beautiful trees.

The view over the Bodstedt Bodden from the living room on the ground floor, the Bodden room on the upper floor and the garden facing south is wonderful. Many historical architectural elements – façade, windows, doors, stairs and floors – have been restored preserving their historic character and were supplemented by new fixtures and furniture as well as modern technology, so that guests feel very comfortable in its historic rooms.

The Kapitänshaus with its 5 bedrooms offers enough space for up to 8 people. In the ground floor there is a living room around the central kitchen that is divided into two areas - reading at the fire-place and/or television -, a corridor with spacious wardrobe, two bedrooms, pantry, a generous bathroom with housekeeping room and in the extension the large windowed dining room with direct access to the garden. The beautiful old wooden staircase leads to the upper floor and the bright central hallway offers a further retreat or play area and three bedrooms, a bathroom with shower and a sauna.

Exterior view. View of the living room.

A bedroom. Staircase. Interior view of the kitchen and dining room. Plan of the ground floor.

GETTING AROUND. THE FISCHLAND-DARSS-ZINGST PENINSULA IS ONE OF THE MOST ATTRACTIVE HOLIDAY DESTINATIONS ON THE GERMAN BALTIC COAST. THE NATIONAL PARK WITH ITS WILD AND ROMANTIC WESTERN BEACH IS ALL YEAR ROUND A POPULAR DESTINATION FOR NATURE LOVERS LOOKING FOR RELAXATION. IN THE QUIET BODDEN VILLAGE OF WIECK YOU CAN ENJOY A WONDERFUL HOLIDAY WITH THE CLEANEST AIR AND AWAY FROM TOURIST CROWDS. SOME POSSIBLE ACTIVITIES ARE SWIMMING, CYCLING, SAILING, SURFING, HIKING, HORSE RIDING. THE WORLD HERITAGE CITY OF STRALSUND IS ONLY A SHORT DISTANCE AWAY.

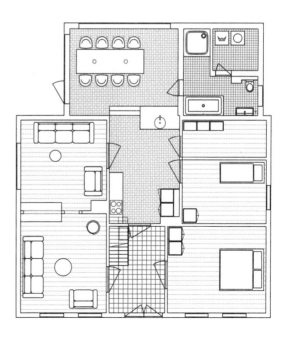

REFUGIUM
ein Ort,
an den man sich gern zurückzieht,
um Ruhe zu haben.

Der "BETZ" (fränkisch)
Das SCHAF

INFORMATION. ARCHITECTS>
BUCHER | HÜTTINGER - ARCHITEKTUR
INNEN ARCHITEKTUR // 2017. TWO
HOLIDAY HOMES> 45 SQM EACH +
30 SQM TERRACE // 2 GUESTS
EACH // 1 BEDROOM EACH //
1 BATHROOM EACH. ADDRESS>
METZENBÜHLSTRASSE 6,
BETZENSTEIN, NÜRNBERG, BAVARIA.
WWW.BIO-DESIGN-FERIENWOHNUN-
GEN.DE

*Interior view living room. Sourroundings.
Side view. View from the garden.*

Refugium Betzenstein

BETZENSTEIN, BAVARIA

Architecture and design are in perfect harmony with nature. The architecture of the elongated building with its striking double saddle roof is based on the topographical conditions and traditional forms and materials of the local environment. They have been architecturally reinvented using modern tools. Embedded in a northern slope, the structure blends unobtrusively into the surrounding hilly landscape with rocks and beech forests. The roof and façade appear as a monolithic structure, completely even and as if cast in one piece. The dark shingles respectfully take up the regional building tradition of slate from Upper Franconia. The architectural language is minimalist with reduction to the essentials and cautious choice of materials and colors. The holiday apartments combine natural building materials with a modern designlanguage and a scope for surprising combinations. The natural landscaping with native trees, orchards and Jurassic limestone reflects the typical landscape of the Franconian Switzerland Nature Park. The Refugium is a place close to nature to retreat and enjoy peace and silence. Nestled in a magnificent natural landscape, the organic holiday home offers healthy living and electrosmog-free design apartments. This is the perfect place to experience a relaxing holiday in the countryside while contributing to sustainability. Following the example of nature, the passive house has been built with the consistent use of regenerative, healthy and environmentally friendly building materials.

Front view. A bedroom. Detail of the living room.
The ground floor plan.

GETTING AROUND. THE NATURE PARK FRANCONIAN SWITZERLAND COVERS THE ENTIRE REGION OF THE NORTHERN FRANKENJURA MOUNTAINS IN BAVARIA. FAR AWAY FROM STRESS AND MAD RUSH, THE REGION OFFERS A WIDE VARIETY OF LEISURE ACTIVITIES: FROM CLIMBING, CANOEING AND CYCLING, TO TAILORMADE THEME HIKES AND CULTURAL EXPERIENCES. AS THE REGION WITH THE HIGHEST DENSITY OF BREWERIES AND DISTILLERIES IN THE WORLD, FRANCONIA'S SWITZERLAND IS KNOWN FOR ITS UNIQUE CULINARY SPECIALTIES. FURTHERMORE, IT IS ONE OF THE MOST FAMOUS REGIONS WITH FORTIFIED CASTLES IN CENTRAL EUROPE.

INFORMATION. ARCHITECTS> THOMAS KRÖGER ARCHITEKTEN // 2014. HOLIDAY HOME> 320 SQM + 97 SQM GUEST HOUSE // 11 GUESTS + 4 GUESTS IN THE GUEST HOUSE // 5 BEDROOMS + 2 BEDROOMS IN THE GUEST HOUSE // 3 BATHROOMS + 1 BATHROOM WITH SEPERATE TOILET IN THE GUEST HOUSE. ADDRESS> ORT FERGITZ 7, GERSWALDE, BRANDENBURG. WWW.LANDHAUS-FERGITZ.COM

Landhaus Fergitz

GERSWALDE, BRANDENBURG

In a small village in the heart of the Uckermark region, north of Berlin, a large barn was converted into a country home with a separate holiday apartment. The barn was built 140 years ago of a mixed construction of brickwork and timber work. Once the junker, the former owner, had been expelled from his land and it had been devided up, two settler families took over the property. Architect Thomas Kröger converted one half of the house for a young family in a way that its original style could easily match with the new design rules and resources. Together with the barn, this former cowshed is an extremely solid building with thick stone walls, small windows and a large wooden gate. A double-height living hall with a fireplace constitutes the center of the house. Three new arched openings with massive wooden gates offer a great view on beautiful fruit trees and the green surrounding landscape. The large hall is not heated but surrounded by a closed, heated body. This means that, instead, only the smaller and more convivial areas of the house can be used in the cold seasons, similar to bird's nests. The conversion of the building shell brought new openings to the private garden and connected the interior and exterior space.

Open kitchen and dining area. Interior view of the main house. View from the garden. Living room.

Garden view by night. Detail of the wooden structure. Bathroom. Ground flloor and first floor plans. View of the dining area.

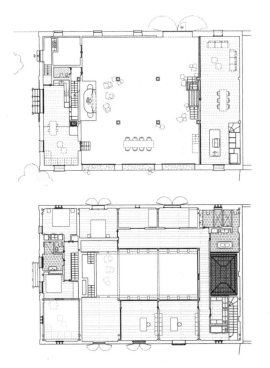

GETTING AROUND. THE COUNTRY HOUSE IS SITUATED AT THE EDGE OF THE SMALL VILLAGE FERGITZ IN THE HILLY TERMINAL MORAINE LANDSCAPE OF THE NORTHERN UCKERMARK REGION. THE SMALL BEACH OF FERGITZ ON THE WEST SHORE OF LAKE OBERUCKERSEE IS ONLY 10 MINUTES WALK FROM THE HOUSE AND CAN BE REACHED VIA AN IDYLLIC COUNTRY LANE. FERGITZ ITSELF IS LOCATED NORTH IN THE BIOSPHERE RESERVE SCHORF-HEIDE-CHORIN. THIS AREA IS ONE OF THE MOST BEAUTIFUL LANDSCAPES OF GERMANY ESPECIALLY FOR NATURE LOVERS, HIKERS, CANOEISTS AND CYCLISTS.

INFORMATION. ARCHITECT>
BRUNE ARCHITEKTUR // 2013.
HOTEL> 35 ROOMS AND
APARTMENTS, FROM 21 TO 75 SQM
// 88 GUESTS // 35 BEDROOMS // 35
BATHROOMS. ADDRESS> DAMENPFAD
37–40,NORDERNEY, LOWER SAXONY.
WWW.INSELLOFT-NORDERNEY.DE

Inselloft
Norderney

NORDERNEY, LOWER SAXONY

The Inselloft Norderney holiday homes consist of four independent and listed houses dating from the turn of the century. It combines beautiful stucco work with modern glass fronts. The solid wood planks, turned woods and natural stone floors made of Belgian blue stone are particularly impressive. They stand in contrast to the wall panels made of rough sawn wood. Each loft is unique because of its long tradition and satisfies high standards in comfort and furnishings. All rooms have large bathrooms with natural stone, many of them have a bathtub and a separate shower. Some of the open kitchens are equipped with a dishwasher and an inviting sitting area, thus guests can have an extensive brunch (except in the studio).

Whether a loft bed or kitchen, a walk-in wardrobe or everything in one! Many of the lofts with a ceiling height of up to three meters contain built-in cubes, which offer a sleeping possibility in the upper area. A small staircase leads up to the upper area. Underneath there is a storage space for holiday outfits or a kitchen, but in any case every cube gives the lofts a very stylish structure.

View into the penthouse. Duplex Maxi-Loft.
View of the veranda. Evening mood.

*Back of the Inselloft. Interior view of
the cube. Floor plans of the maisonnette
and floor plan of the loft. Bathroom.*

GETTING AROUND. IT ONLY TAKES A FEW STEPS FROM THE LOFT TO THE LIMIT LINE OF THE HIGH TIDE. THE PLACE TO BE OF NORDENEY ISLAND – THE MILCHBAR – IS IN DIRECT NEIGHBOURHOOD AND OFFERS RELAXED SOUNDS, COOL DRINKS AND THE BEST SUNSETS OF THE ISLAND. THE BEST CAKE IS SERVED AT THE MARIENHÖHE. THE STRIKING COPPER ROOF OF THE PAVILION SHINES FROM AFAR ON THE HOHE DÜNE. THE HOLIDAY DAY ENDS IN THE EVENING IN THE MICHELIN-STARRED RESTAURANT ON THE PIER AT THE SEASIDE. A GLASS FRONT OPENS UP THE VIEW TO THE CHEFS IN THE SHOW KITCHEN BEFORE THE ISLAND STYLE DISHES ARE SERVED.

INFORMATION. ARCHITECTS>
BJÖRN GÖTTE, MARKUS STÖCKLEIN //
2017. HOLIDAY HOME> 70 SQM +
24 SQM SAUNA // UP TO 6 GUESTS //
2 BEDROOMS // 1 BATHROOM.
ADDRESS> WICHMANNSDORF,
KRÖPELIN, MECKLENBURG-WESTERN
POMERANIA.
WWW.FINCA-BALTICA.DE

View of the dining and kitchen area.
Entrance area. View from the garden.

Finca Baltica

KRÖPELIN,
MECKLENBURG-WESTERN
POMERANIA

Finca Baltica is located next to Kühlungsborn, Rerik and Heiligendamm in one of the most beautiful landscapes of the coast of Mecklenburg-Western Pomerania, the socalled Kühlung. It is situated at the edge of fields and meadows, right behind the village of Kühlungsborn, in the romantic little village of Wichmannsdorf. Finca Baltica belongs to a 3,700-square-meter property with wild trees, flowering bushes, strawberries, cherries and sloes. It is a perfect hideaway for families and friends.

The house's architecture and design are convincing, not only because of its large window front that opens up a panoramic view and allows cooling. The spacious wooden terrace meshes the living space with nature. The view of the beautiful nature is stunning, not only in summer. The living room has a fireplace and a fully equipped kitchen. Two separate bedrooms invite to dream, the little ones enjoy playing in the big garden or having fun in the Strandhaus beach house. Up to six people can find a temporary home here.

GETTING AROUND. THE FINCA IS ONLY 5 KM AWAY FROM THE BEACH OF KÜHLUNGSBORN. THE SEA CAN BE REACHED QUICKLY BY BIKE OR CAR. EXCURSIONS TO HEILIGENDAMM OR RERIK – BOTH PLACES ARE A CAT'S JUMP AWAY FROM WICHMANNS-DORF – ARE A BEAUTIFUL LEISURE ACTIVITY, SO ARE HORSE RIDING, GOLFING, SWIMMING, HIKING OR BICYCLE TOURS. THE DAY ENDS AT THE FIREPLACE OR IN THE SAUNA HOUSE WITH THE SUNSET OVER THE ADJOINING FIELDS.

Exterior view of the sauna. Terrace.
A bunk bed in the bedroom.

Interior view of the kitchen.
Bedroom. Terrace.

INFORMATION. ENGINEER>
PETER BLÜMEL, MALCHOW // 2016.
MANOR HOUSE AND OTHER
BUILDINGS > 1,000 SQM // 46 GUESTS
// 23 BEDROOMS // 21 BATHROOMS.
ADDRESS> DORFSTRASSE 29-30,
LEXOW, WALOW, MECKLENBURG-
WESTERN POMERANIA.
WWW.GUTSHAUS-LEXOW.DE

*View from the garden. Bathroom with
the original furniture. Dining area.
Common living space with fireplace.*

Gutshaus Lexow

WALOW,
MECKLENBURG-WESTERN
POMERANIA

Guthaus Lexow was built in 1874. During the GDR era, the building was used as supermarket, school, medical practice and dwelling. After the fall of communism, it stood empty for many years until Bettina Buschow and Patrick Oldendorf bought it in 2007 and began to renovate it carefully.

At first, they built three large holiday apartments, and in the following years they added further apartments and B&B rooms in the old kitchen annex, which had also been renovated. The cartwright was rebuilt in 2016 and the ensemble has now room for a total of 46 guests in six holiday apartments and eight double rooms.

Each unit of the manor house is furnished with loving care and style. The apartments offer a lot of space to spend time together or to withdraw. Well-equipped kitchens allow cooking together, fireplaces and stoves promise cozy evenings. All rooms are individually designed. Breakfast, coffee and dinner are served in the small guest room, usually based on local ingredients. On request, catering can be arranged for groups. Companies and their employees will find a homely, informal and yet productive and inspiring environment for workshops, celebrations or other events.

*Bedroom with en-suite
bathroom. Garden view.*

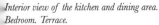

Interior view of the kitchen and dining area.
Bedroom. Terrace.

GETTING AROUND. THE GUTSHAUS LEXOW IS SITUATED IN THE HEART OF THE MECKLENBURG LAKE REGION, SURROUNDED BY MEADOWS, FORESTS AND FIELDS. THE MOST BEAUTIFUL AND HIDDEN SPOT FOR SWIMMING AT THE GROSSER KRESSIN SEE IS 3 KM AWAY AND OTHER LAKES LIKE MÜRITZ, PLAUER SEE AND FLEESENSEE ARE EACH ABOUT 8 KILOMETRES AWAY. ROEBEL, WAREN AND THE MÜRITZ ARE EACH APPROX. AT A DISTANCE OF 15 KM. THE REGION OFFERS A BEAUTIFUL, DIVERSE LANDSCAPE INCLUDING THE MÜRITZ NATIONAL PARK AND MANY EXCITING MUSEUMS, MONUMENTS AND ANCIENT CHURCHES.

INFORMATION. CONCEPT>
MARK POHL // 2012. HOLIDAY
APARTMENTS> 250 SQM // 16 GUESTS
// 6 BEDROOMS // 3 BATHROOMS.
ADDRESS> FULDAER STRASSE 85,
WEIMAR, THURINGIA.
WWW.HIERWARGOETHENIE.DE

Bedroom. View through the corridor.
Workstation and living room.

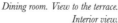
Dining room. View to the terrace.
Interior view.

Design Apartments Weimar

WEIMAR, THURINGIA

The unique concept of the Design Apartments Weimar combines holiday, design and shopping. Mark Pohl and Udo Joerke are running this three new holiday apartments dating from 2012. They are located in an ensemble of monuments that was built in 1907 and refurbished to a high standard and accurate to every detail between 2009 and 2011. The original condition of the building was brought to life thanks to the materials that were used and to the careful handling of the structure.

The existing wooden windows, the solid wood plank flooring and the loam plaster of the walls were renovated and the rooms furnished with modern elements. Guests can stay in the rooftop apartment of 50 square meters or in two 105-square-meters apartments with loggia and balcony. The interior design of the apartment consists of a mixture of design classics, flea market objects and modern designs, including products by graduates of the Bauhaus University Weimar. The Design Apartments Weimar are like a living showroom, where guests can take a break trying out the furnishings and purchase them on site or online. The aim of the managers is to present affordable design in small series and unique pieces, including finds and handmade design objects. At the same time, the accomodation is meant to make guests feel at home in a friendly and cozy ambience and to inspire them by offering temporary events such as workshops, cooking nights or pop-up shops.

Living area of the studio apartment.
Interior view of the reading corner.

Bedroom with blue walls.
Roof terrace. Floor plan.

GETTING AROUND. WEIMAR IS THE
BIRTHPLACE OF THE BAUHAUS AND
HOME TO THE FAMOUS WRITERS
GOETHE AND SCHILLER, AND WAS
THE EUROPEAN CITY OF CULTURE
IN 1999. BESIDES THE HISTORIC
MEANING, WEIMAR OFFERS
BEAUTIFUL LANDSCAPES. NEXT
DOOR TO THE APARTMENTS
EMERGED NEW STORE CONCEPTS
SUCH AS THE SHOP DESIGNWE.LOVE
FOR LOCAL DESIGN, THE MIXED
CROWD BAR HINTERZIMMER, THE
BAKERY DIE BROTKLAPPE OR THE
LORIAT KUCHENMANUFAKTUR.

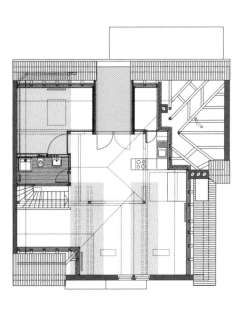

INFORMATION. ARCHITECTS> JÜRGEN FETT, NORBERT MARIA BRAUN HOTELMARKETING GRUPPE // 2015. CHALET AND HOLIDAY HOMES> 75 SQM // 4 + 1 GUESTS // 2 BEDROOMS // 1 BATHROOM WITH SEPARATE WC. ADDRESS> IHLEFELDER STRASSE, MÜLVERSTEDT, THURINGIA. WWW.HAINICHHOEFE.DE

Open kitchen and living room. View to the terrace.
A bedroom. Interior view of the living room.

Hainichhöfe

MÜLVERSTEDT, THURINGIA.

The Hainichhöfe first-class chalets are located in the immediate vicinity of the Hainich National Park. They are nestled in a wonderful natural setting, idyllically situated on a small hill just a few meters from the impressive beech forest. In these cozy chalets life is in harmony with unspoilt nature. No matter what you are looking for: whether peace, space for concentrated work or reflection, exercise in the fresh air or to experience culinary delights and culture around the houses - in the Hainichhöfe guests will find their holiday home, welcoming them to timeout from everyday life and making them continue dreaming even months later.

The holiday home is a good seventy square meters large, lovingly made of regional materials. It offers space for up to four people. There is an extra bed in the living room. A fully equipped open kitchen with dining area offers the possibility to prepare small delicacies from regional ingredients. A wonderful fireplace provides a pleasant cosy warmth. The bathroom has an infrared sauna and is though the perfect place to relax. On the surrounding terrace there is a cooling outdoor shower. Here the guests feel free and light. Arrived in a silence that can hardly be more alive.

View from the garden.
A bedroom in the first floor.

Top view of the living room. Living room with fireplace. Bathroom. Floorplans.

GETTING AROUND. INTENSIVE NATURE EXPERIENCES COMBINED WITH UNIQUE CULTURAL EXPERIENCES? THE WARTBURG CASTLE IS LOCATED IN THE IMMEDIATE NEIGHBOURHOOD NEXT TO THE BEECH FORESTS OF THE HAINICH, A WORLD CULTURAL HERITAGE OF SPECIAL IMPORTANCE. CITIES AND TOWNS SUCH AS WEIMAR, ARNSTADT, EISENACH, ERFURT, GOTHA AND MUELHAUSEN ATTRACT VISITORS WITH THEIR HISTORY, THEIR MONUMENTS AND ROMANTIC CHRISTMAS MARKETS.

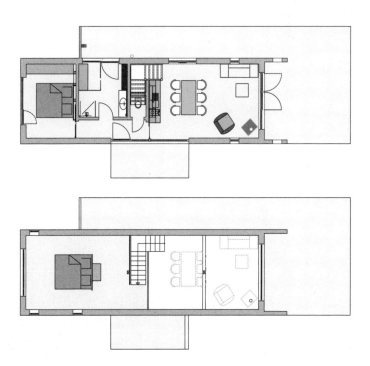

INFORMATION. ARCHITECT>
HANS SCHAROUN // 1933.
HOUSE> 480 SQM // 12 GUESTS //
4 BEDROOMS // 2 BATHROOMS.
ADDRESS> KIRSCHALLEE 1B, LÖBAU,
SAXONY.
WWW.STIFTUNG-HAUSSCHMINKE.EU

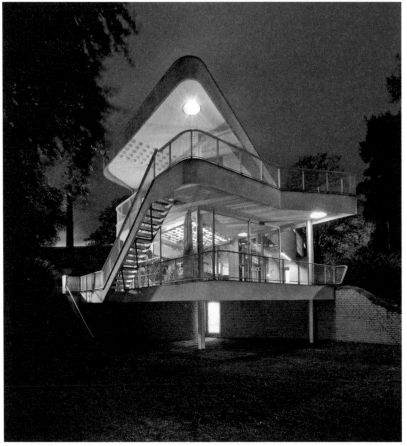

Haus Schminke

LÖBAU, SAXONY.

Haus Schminke by Hans Scharoun located in Löbau, Saxony, is worldwide one of the most important residential buildings of the movement Neues Bauen (new building) and is considered to be one of the most child-friendly houses of its time. Originally designed for a couple of factory owners and their four children, the house today welcomes museum guests from all over the world. Hans Scharoun created "the house I loved most" in Löbau. The elongated building with its curves, terraces, outside stairs, the mighty chimney and the portholes evokes associations with a ship. To this day, the house bears the affectionate nickname "noodle steamer". The flowing rooms offer a unique quality of living due to the interplay between house and garden. The large windows and the airy, light-flooded atmosphere blur the boundaries between inside and outside. After it has been closed for visitors, Haus Schminke offers the unique opportunity to enjoy the architecture exclusively within the framework of an overnight stay starting in the early evening. Guests can choose from seven beds in four rooms. A total of twelve people can stay overnight and enjoy the fully equipped kitchen as well as the huge garden with barbecue and fire place.

View from the garden. Exterior view by night.
Main entrance. Interior view of the kitchen.

Dining room with garden view. Detail of the conservatory. View from garden. Floor plans. South-East view by night

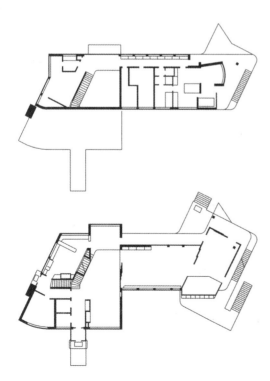

GETTING AROUND. IN OBER-LAUSITZ BETWEEN DRESDEN AND GÖRLITZ, THE PROJECT TOPOMOMO PRESENTS MANY EXAMPLAREY BUILDINGS OF THE MODERNIST ERA WHICH ARE RATHER UNKNOWN. THE INNER CITIES OF LÖBAU, KAMENZ, BAUTZEN, GÖRLITZ AND ZITTAU REFLECT ALSO THE GLORIOUS PAST OF THE MEDIEVAL SIX-CITIES FEDERATION. THE ZITTAU AND THE GIANT MOUNTAINS IN THE GERMAN-POLISH-CZECH BORDER AREA ARE A WONDERFUL HIKING REGION. WWW.TOPOMOMO.EU

INFORMATION. ARCHITECTS> PETER GRUNDMANN, MARTIN HANSEN AND MARIEKEN VERHEYEN // 2015. ENSEMBLE OF HOUSES, BARN, STABLE AND GARDEN HOUSES> 2 HA // 3 TO 5 GUESTS PER APARTMENT // 8 BEDROOMS // 8 BATHROOMS. ADDRESS> DORFSTRASSE 23, LYCHEN, BRANDENBURG. WWW.REHOF-RUTENBERG.DE

View from the terrace to the bedroom. Staircase.

Re:hof Rutenberg

LYCHEN, BRANDENBURG

With the conversion of the parsonage and its beautiful old grown garden into Re:hof Rutenberg, a form of holidays in the country side is offered which many people may wish for, but rarely find. This is a place to rediscover the simplicity of life while enjoying it in comfort and freedom from everything superfluous.

"Back to basics." What does a person need to be happy? Marieken Verheyen and Martin Hansen have always been asking themselves this question during the conversion of the farm – and this is exactly why the name Re:hof was created: Re: in the sense of new again. Together with the architect Peter Grundmann they were able to implement the ambitious concept.

In the middle of the most beautiful nature, guests will find many different holiday apartments: generously designed lofts in the former stable, interesting pavilions in the garden between the old fruit trees, a wheelchair-accessible apartment in the farmhouse and a modern romantic holiday apartment in the parsonage. The Re:hof guests not only have the apartments with their mainly natural look at their disposal, but also the entire grounds: the old parish garden with fruit and vegetables, the sauna, several terraces and fireplaces and the large barn, the Hotel for special occasions and events. The farm shop offers tasty organic products and wines, as well as homemade products from the farm's own garden.

View of the garden shed "Sali".
Interior view of "Lupulus".

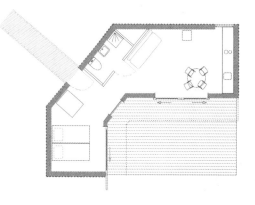

GETTING AROUND. THE NATURE PARK UCKERMÄRKISCHE SEEN (LAKES) BEGINS RIGHT BEHIND THE TWO HECTARE SITE. IT IS CHARACTERIZED BY EXTENSIVE FORESTS, MEADOWS, FIELDS AND LAKES – A TYPICAL TERMINAL MORAINE LANDSCAPE. THE GROSSER KRONSEE, ONE OF THE CLEAREST LAKES OF THE REGION, IS LOCATED AT THE EDGE OF THE VILLAGE. RUTENBERG IS SITUATED ON THE CYCLE ROUTE UCKERMÄRKISCHER FAHRRADRUNDWEG, WHICH OFFERS PLENTY OF DIFFERENT POSSIBILITIES OF CYCLING TOURS IN EVERY DIRECTION. FROM LYCHEN YOU CAN ALSO TAKE A CANOE FOR EXCITING TRIPS AND JOURNEYS ACROSS THE SEVEN SURROUNDING LAKES.

Kitchen and living area. Floor plans.
Exterior view of "Lupulus".

Kitchen area with sleeping alcoves.
Exterior view. View from the garden by night.

INFORMATION. ARCHITECT> BERND VORDERMEIER // 2017. HOLIDAY HOME> 80 SQM // 9 GUESTS // 2 BEDROOMS // 2 BATHROOMS. ADDRESS> MOOSHAM 13, GRAFENAU, BAVARIA. WWW.MOOSHAM13.COM

Interior view of the living room. Staircase. View of the north front from the garden.

Moosham 13

GRAFENAU, BAVARIA

Verena Windorfer-Bogner and Reinhold Windorfer are the seventh generation to manage the Moosham 13 farm, which consists of a home, a stable and outbuildings as well as a listed bread oven. Both dreamed of a sustainable, robust and high-quality renovation with a modern and reduced design for their house, built around 1840.

The staircase to the tower was extended in order to access the attic floor that was converted into a living space. Two new apartments have been built and can be booked separately or together and offer space for up to nine guests. The use of this space is manifold because the structure was optimized by placing cubes for the sanitary rooms in a central position. Moosham 13 is a holiday home for individuals and couples, families and friends, or even a place of retreat during creative workshops. The pleasant indoor climate comes from the wood-fired heating system in the envelopping surface that is fired with own logs, from the natural lime plaster, ecological building materials and the self-made floor planks from their private forest.

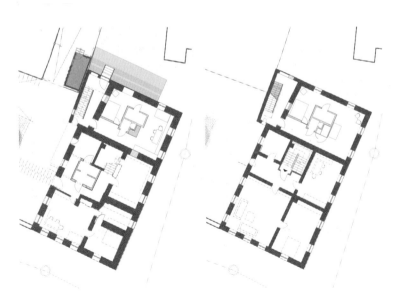

GETTING AROUND. MOOSHAM 13 IS LOCATED IN THE IMMEDIATE VICINITY OF THE BAVARIAN FOREST NATIONAL PARK, THE OLDEST ONE IN GERMANY. IN THIS UNIQUE, UNTOUCHED NATURAL LANDSCAPE THERE ARE NUMEROUS HIKING, MOUNTAIN BIKING AND CROSS-COUNTRY SKIING ROUTES. FURTHER ACTIVITIES ARE, FOR EXAMPLE, THE VISIT OF THE WILDLIFE PARK WITH ANIMALS AND THE TREETOP PATH IN NEU-SCHÖNAU, THE OPEN-AIR MUSEUM IN FINSTERAU OR TRIPS TO THE CZECH REPUBLIC OR TO AUSTRIA

Open space with kitchen, living and dining area.
Floor plans. View of the terrace.

Bedroom. Interior view of the
modern staircase. The large atelier space
on the second upper floor.

INFORMATION. ARCHITECT>
RUDOLF RECHL // 2015.
MEDIEVAL TOWER WITH HOLIDAY
APARTMENTS> 500 SQM //
25 GUESTS // 11 BEDROOMS //
7 BATHROOMS. ADDRESS>
SCHEDLING 4, TROSTBERG, BAVARIA.
WWW.SCHLOSS-SCHEDLING.DE

Living space on several floors. Bathtub with garden view. Dining corner. Exterior view of the tower.

Turm zu Schloss Schedling

TROSTBERG, BAVARIA

The medieval tower with its six exclusive holiday apartments was built next to Schedling Castle on the edge of the historic old town of Trostberg an der Alz. The three Stubn (rooms) in the tower offer unforgettable holidays for couples. Guests immerse in the apartments' romantic ambience through beautiful four-poster beds, charming tiled stoves, historic vaults, luxurious bathrooms with rain showers and picturesque outdoor sitting areas or idyllic gardens. Each of the three "palaces" guarantees a very special holiday experience, no matter if romantic or not, as a couple or with the whole family.

Discover the labyrinthine rooms on different floors, open fireplaces in the living area or on the patio, eye-catching tiled stove towers, cozy four-poster beds, exclusive bathrooms with whirlpools and rain shower, quiet patios or gardens with splashing fountains made of natural stone. A special highlight for little guests is their own kingdom in the prince palace with cozy sleeping caves and a mysterious secret passage.

The vacation day ends with candlelight on outdoor seats on warm summer evenings, while on cool autumn and winter evenings the pleasent tiled stove warmth the accommodation.

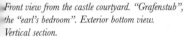
Front view from the castle courtyard. "Grafenstub",
the "earl's bedroom". Exterior bottom view.
Vertical section.

GETTING AROUND. TROSTBERG IS SITUATED BETWEEN MUNICH AND SALZBURG IN THE BEAUTIFUL LANDSCAPE OF THE CHIEMGAU, ONLY A QUARTER OF AN HOUR AWAY FROM, THE CHIEMSEE LAKE. THE CHIEMGAU IS WORTH A VISIT AT ANY TIME OF THE YEAR. DISCOVER THE LAKE AND THE ALPS OF CHIEMGAU, IDYLLIC HIKING AND BIKING TRAILS, WONDERFUL RIVERS AND LAKES, OLD CASTLES AND FORTRESSES, NUMEROUS GOLF COURSES IN THE AREA, WINTER SPORTS AND WELLNESS PROGRAMMES AND A WIDE RANGE OF CULTURAL EVENTS.

INFORMATION. ARCHITECT>
GÖTZ OERTEL // 2013.
5 HOLIDAY APARTMENTS> 250 SQM //
10 GUESTS, 2 GUESTS EACH
APARTMENT // 1 BEDROOM EACH //
1 BATHROOM EACH.
ADDRESS> OBERSTRASSE 30,
SIMMERN, RHINELAND-PALATINATE.
WWW.SOON-APPARTEMENTS.DE

View of the bedroom from the living room.
Front view. Living room. Bedroom.

SOON
Appartements

SIMMERN, RHINELAND-PALATINATE

SOON Apartments. These are five modern holiday apartments plus a conference room in a quiet location in the pedestrian zone of Simmern in the foothills of the Hunsrück – surrounded by restaurants, cafés and shops. The holiday apartments contain a mix of design furniture and vintage originals and are decorated in cooperation with Pro-Winzkino e.V. with stills from Edgar Reitz's films about his homeland. The roof terrace offers a beautiful view of the countryside as well as the tower Schinderhannesturm and the church Stephanskirche. Situated in the quiet rear part of the house, two 60-square-meter apartments on the 1st and 2nd floors of the house are oriented towards the courtyards and gardens of the Oberstraße. A well-protected terrace or a small balcony offer a place of privacy where, for instance, guests may enjoy a

good book. The open room concept creates a light and friendly atmosphere. A total of three smaller studios, each with a surface of 26 to30 square meters, are face to face to the pedestrian zone. The two larger studios in the 1st and 2nd floors have large windows and furniture in light colors what makes the atmosphere clear and friendly. The smallest studio apartment in the top floor of the house with its dormer windows, the old floorboards and the high ceilings exudes a special charm. The 60-square-metre roof terrace is the perfect place to enjoy the sun and the view of the Stephanskirche church as well as the Schinderhannesturm tower. The seminar room on the ground floor offers space for meetings as well as cooking and wine evenings.

Open dining area and bedroom. Roof terrace.

Common room. Bedroom.
First floor ground plan.

GETTING AROUND. FRESH AIR TO TAKE DEEP BREATHS, PEACE TO RELAX AND STARS TO DREAM – IT'S ALL THERE IN THE HUNSRÜCK, JUST AN HOUR'S DRIVE FROM FRANKFURT AND AN HOUR AND A HALF FROM COLOGNE. HIKERS WILL FIND RELAXATION ON THE FANTASTIC FIRST-CLASS HIKING TRAIL SOONWALDSTEIG. THE MOST FAMOUS SIGHT IN HUNSRÜCK IS PROBABLY THE SUSPENSION BRIDGE GEIERLAY, GERMANY'S LONGEST SUSPENSION BRIDGE. IT IS A FACT THAT CULTURAL DIVERSITY EXISTS IN THE COUNTRYSIDE, TOO: THE MUSEUM OF LOCAL HISTORY SHOWS CHANGING EXHIBITIONS, THERE ARE ART STUDIOS AND GALLERIES TO EXPLORE AS WELL AS A LOT OF CONCERTS AND OTHER EVENTS TO VISIT.

INFORMATION. ARCHITECT>
FLORIAN NAGLER // 2012. NATURE
HOTEL & HEALTH RESORT> FROM 9
TO 36 SQM PER ROOM // 100 GUESTS
// 60 BEDROOMS // 60 BATHROOMS.
ADDRESS> TANNERHOFSTRASSE 32,
BAYRISCHZELL, BAVARIA.
WWW.TANNERHOF.DE

Bottom view. Hut tower and sourroundings.
Terrace from the top. Garden view.
Bedroom with private balcony.

Tannerhof

BAYRISCHZELL, BAVARIA

A normal, relaxed atmosphere, the coexistence of young and old, of sound and silence, of spirits and herbal tea. The Tannerhof oscillates between hotel, health, organic gourmet cuisine, culture and nature. It is ambiguous, artistic, loving. Holiday, health, therapeutic fasting, 5-course menu, rooms of 9 to 36 square meters, old, new, high culture, greenhouse, high heels and walking barefoot. No clowning around, no livery.

Concernig the following the Tannerhof architecture and philosophy are exceptionally strict: everyone lives in its own way. What sounds like a cliché makes the Tannerhof an inspiring place – it is avantgarde in its authenticity. On the one hand simple, almost naive, lovingly quirky and digitally slowed down.

Design comes from the heart and not from the PC. However, architect Florian Nagler introduced modernity at its best: cautious respect for the existing buildings that have grown over generations. The subtle, elegant architectural framing of buildings from different eras even reinforce the heart of the building – the venerable farming house Alte Tann. Both of Nagler's hut towers from 2012 are contemporary neighboors next to hermit's huts from 1905 and they are complementary, not dominant. The architectural coexistence outdoors joins the Tannerhof philosophy indoors.

View from the garden at night.
General view of the Tannerhof.

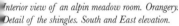
Interior view of an alpin meadow room. Orangery.
Detail of the shingles. South and East elevation.

GETTING AROUND. THE TANNER-
HOF IS NESTLED ON A SLOPE ABOVE
BAYRISCHZELL – WITH A VIEW ON THE
WENDELSTEIN MOUNTAIN AND THE
SUDELFELD MOUNTAINS IN THE BACK.
IN SUMMER, HIKING, CYCLING, PARA-
GLIDING. SWIMMING IN THE SCHLIER-
SEE, THIERSEE OR THE TEGERNSEE.
IN WINTER ENDLESS KILOMETERS
OF CROSS-COUNTRY TRAILS IN BAY-
RISCHZELL AND FISCHBACHAU,
THE SKI RESORTS SUDELFELD AND
SPITZINGSEE. MUNICH'S CULTURE,
SIGHTSEEING IN SALZBURG, THE
KUFSTEIN ROUND THE CORNER. THE
FELLOW VALUE PRODUCERS IN THE
COUNTRY. AND ALWAYS: COMING
BACK TO THE HOLIDAY HOME. LYING
UNDER THE TREES AND READING.
HAVING A LOOK ON THE FIRE IN THE
CHIMNEY LOUNGE AND PLAYING THE
FAVORITE SONG ON THE WURLITZER...

INFORMATION. ARCHITECTS> WACKER ZEIGER ARCHITEKTEN // 2008. HOLIDAY HOME> 75 SQM // 2 BEDROOMS // 2 BATHROOMS. ADDRESS> STRASSE ZUM MEER 10, LUBMIN, MECKLENBURG-WESTERN POMERANIA. WWW.OSTSEE-URLAUB-LUBMIN.DE

Exterior view. View of the entry.
External perspective.

Meerhaus Lubmin

LUBMIN,
MECKLENBURG-WESTERN
POMERANIA

This small wooden holiday home stands under pine trees and offers a view on the Baltic Sea. Contrary to the architecture imitating that of Heiligendamm next door, it maintains a more modest but at the same time self-confident "dacha culture".

The construction consists of wooden panels covered with a vertical larch curtain. In the area of the terraced undercut, the façade consists of rusty steel plates from a nearby shipyard. The flat sloping roof has a standing seam covering in zinc. The windows with narrow frames are positioned in the façade in such a way that the closed and open surfaces together create a tension. The building has two levels and can accommodate up to 6 people. Meerhaus Lubmin has an open floor plan where the gallery-like attic is facing the ground floor.

The interior walls and ceilings are white. The screed of the floor is painted in grey. Because of their construction structure the solid wood frames (KVH) of the wooden panels (16 centimeters external walls, 20 centimeters roof ceiling) provide optimal conditions for good thermal insulation, which is reflected by visibly low heating consumption. The floor heating is operated with an air heat pump. Since the holiday home is not always inhabited, the heat pump is mainly used out of season to maintain a basic temperature. During the months of transition and also on cold days during the season, a soapstone stove heats the house.

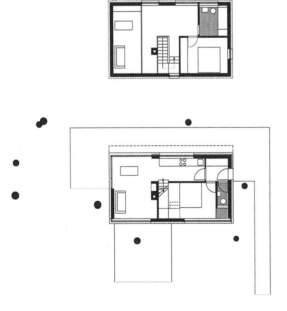

GETTING AROUND. LUBMIN, THE "PEARL AT THE BAY OF GREIFSWALD" (GREIFSWALDER BODDEN), IS A PLACE WITH CLEAN AIR WHERE YOU CAN GO SWIMMING, DIVING, WIND AND KITESURFING, AND TAKE LONG WALKS ALONG THE FINE SANDY BEACH OR IN THE ADJOINING PINE FOREST. ON THE NEARBY "STONE BEACH" THERE IS AN IMPRESSIVE SEVERAL TONS HEAVY "DEVIL'S STONE". IN THE HARBOR YOU WILL FIND FISHING BOATS, FRESHLY CAUGHT AND SMOKED FISH. THE NEW MARINA IS THE IDEAL STARTING POINT FOR EXTENDED SAILING TRIPS. IN THE EVENING THE PIER (SEEBRÜCKE) IS A ROMANTIC PLACE TO GO TO WATCH THE CHANGING SKY SCENERY. BOAT TRIPS INCLUDE KRÖSLIN, THE UNIVERSITY TOWN OF GREIFSWALD AND THE BALTIC SEASIDE RESORTS OF THE ISLANDS OF RÜGEN AND USEDOM.

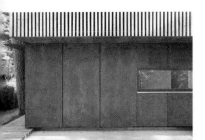

Side view. Floor plans.
Front detail.

View of the terrace. Front view.
View from the garden.

INFORMATION. ARCHITECTS>
ARNOLD / WERNER ARCHITEKTEN //
2014. DESIGN HOTEL> 800 SQM //
31 GUESTS // 16 BEDROOMS //
16 BATHROOMS. ADDRESS>
FRAUNHOFERSTRASSE 32, MUNICH,
BAVARIA.
WWW.FLUSHINGMEADOWSHOTEL.COM

Bedroom. Interior view of the hotel room.
Communal living area with fireplace.

The Flushing Meadows

MUNICH, BAVARIA

The Flushing Meadows is located on the third and fourth floors of a former industrial building from the 1970s. In contrast, it is a rather impressive design hotel of 800 square meters. The eleven loft studios on the lower floor were designed and furnished by Arnold/ Werner together with personalities from the fields of music, drama, design, gastronomy, fashion, sports and arts.

Five penthouse studios were built on the upper floor, some of which have their own roof terrace with a stunning Alpine panorama. These light-flooded rooms impress with their amazing view as well as their high-quality furnishing. All penthouse studios are finished with stained solid wood, fabric-covered walls and copper elements. On top of this, each room has exclusive drawings and paintings by the young Berlin artist

Maximilian Rödel. This project made by enthusiasts combines the rough ambience of the existing building with the customized furnishing and furniture concept creating a unique experience for the guests. Part of the hotel is also a rooftop bar, which invites guests to have breakfast in the morning and to relax and enjoy the Glockenbach district in the evening. In this way, the bar serves as a meeting point for locals and night owls as well as a communication hotspot of the hotel.

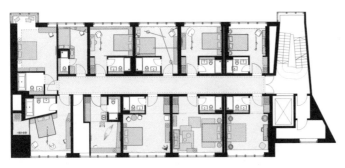

GETTING AROUND. THE DESIGN-HOTEL IS SITUATED IN THE LIVELY GLOCKENBACH DISTRICT OF MUNICH AND IS ONLY A SHORT WALK AWAY FROM THE MARKT SQUARE AND THE OLD PART OF THE CITY. THE NEIGHBORHOOD CONVINCES WITH THE LISTED POST OFFICE BUILDING BY ROBERT VORHÖLZER FROM THE 30S, THE IMMEDIATE PROXIMITY TO THE ISAR, AS WELL AS THE VIBRANT DISTRICT OF GÄRTNERPLATZ. IN ADDITION, THERE IS A VARIETY OF MODERN AND UNIQUE RESTAURANTS, BARS AND SHOPS IN THE IMMEDIATE VICINITY. AS THE UNDERGROUND STATION FRAUNHOFERSTRASSE IS LOCATED DIRECTLY IN FRONT OF THE HOTEL, THE ACCOMMODATION IN THE FLUSHING MEADOWS HOTEL OFFERS A COMFORTABLE CONNECTION TO THE PUBLIC TRANSPORT SYSTEM OF MUNICH.

Interior view of a bedroom.
Floor plans. Detail of a hotel room.

Coffee corner with fireplace and terrace
Bedroom. Hotel room with hammock.

INFORMATION. ARCHITECT>
HANS KNIEPKAMP // 2008.
TWO GUEST HOUSES> 60 AND 52
SQM // 4 GUESTS EACH// OPEN-PLAN
ROOMS // 1 BATHROOM EACH.
ADDRESS> KASTANIENALLEE 21,
PRENZLAUER BERG, BERLIN.
WWW.REMISE-BERLIN.DE

Exterior view of the half-timbered building. Upper floor sleeping area, half-timbered building. Interior view, ground floor, half-timbered building.

Remise Berlin

BERLIN

The Remise is a peaceful hideaway in the heart of the city. A listed ensemble of buildings in the second backyard of Kastanienallee, one of the busiest streets in the central district of Prenzlauer Berg in Berlin. This is an excellent starting point to get to know the city and its history. The ensemble of buildings, which has grown historically since 1891 (main building, stable building, half-timbered building) encloses an inner courtyard, a community and communication platform for the various users of the complex. Currently, a family, a forge for art objects and a software development company live and work in the main building. The stable remise and the half-timbered house are available as guest houses.

It's a good alternative to a hotel. A backyard idyll in the middle of the city. The open plan rooms are decorated with custom furniture designed and built by the architect. Minimalist, simple and clear. The two lovingly furnished guest houses combine city tourism with the experience of an authentic Berlin backyard atmosphere.

GETTING AROUND. NUMEROUS RESTAURANTS, BARS, CAFÉS AND UNUSUAL SHOPS ARE NEXT DOOR. AROUND THE CORNER ARE THE MAUERPARK, THE MEMORIAL OF THE BERLIN WALL, THE KULTURBRAUEREI AND THE LEGENDARY PRATER BIERGARTEN. IT IS THE PERFECT STARTING POINT FOR DISCOVERING THE CITY AND ITS HISTORY. YOU CAN QUICKLY GET TO THE BERLIN'S MITTE DISTRICT AROUND HACKESCHER MARKT. JUST A FEW STEPS AWAY ARE THE MUSEUM ISLAND, FACING THE NEW CASTLE, AND ALEXANDERPLATZ. IT IS VERY EASY TO GET FROM THERE TO ANYWHERE BY PUBLIC TRANSPORT.

View towards the courtyard.
Ground floor. Exterior view of the stable.

Kitchen and dining area, ground
floor, stable. View of the stairway, ground floor,
stable. Upper floor sleeping area, stable.

INFORMATION. ARCHITECTS> PETER DOBELSTEIN, INTERIOR DESIGN> MICHAELA FASOLD AND OLIVER FASOLD// 2016. HOLIDAY HOME> 110 SQM // 6 GUESTS // 3 BEDROOMS // 2 BATHROOMS. ADDRESS> AM KURPARK 21, BREEGE, MECKLENBURG-WESTERN POMERANIA. WWW.LILLESOL.DE

View from the garden. Interior view. Living room with fireplace. Front view.

Lillesol

BREEGE,
MECKLENBURG-WESTERN
POMERANIA

Lillesol is situated on the edge of the peninsula of Wittow in Rügen, not far from the famous lighthouses of Cape Arkona, next to the historic spa gardens of the small seaside resort Juliusruh. The cosy holiday home is only a few minutes away from the fine sandy beach of the Baltic Sea and merges harmoniously with its environment thanks to its reduced and modern Scandinavian design language.

The wooden exterior made of larch, weathered and untreated, communicates perfectly with the 200-year-old lime trees that line the park's path. The architect Peter Dobelstein designed, together with the clients, a light-flooded architectural plan with a gallery, which offers views all the way to the gable and the Kurpark.

The open kitchen and the fireplace are situated in the centre of the room. These elements give the living area its face and make it possible to enjoy the natural play of light and weather through the floor-to-ceiling windows at any time of the year. Three bedrooms and two bathrooms, one of them with sauna, complement the living and dining area in its charming atmosphere. The interior is in harmony because of its holistic color and material concept. The leitmotif of the selection is Italian fine stone slabs, oiled oak and light gray.

 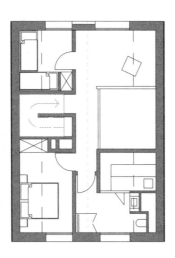

GETTING AROUND. THE HOLIDAY HOUSE LILLESOL IS AN IDEAL STARTING POINT FOR INDIVIDUAL DISCOVERY TRIPS: FROM THE PENINSULA OF WITTOW VIA OLD CHURCHES TO CAPE ARKONA OR TO THE WITTOW FERRY. BUT ALSO THE SCHAABE BEACH, THE VORPOMMERISCHE BODDEN-LANDSCHAFT NATIONAL PARK, ISLAND OF HIDDENSEE AND THE JASMUND NATURE RESERVE ARE ABSOLUTELY WORTH SEEING. THE SOPHISTICATED SEASIDE RESORTS OF BINZ, SELLIN AND GÖHREN CAN BE REACHED BY CAR IN ABOUT HALF AN HOUR AND THE HANSEATIC TOWNS OF STRALSUND AND GRIFFSWALD INVITE VISITORS ON A TRIP.

A bedroom. Floor plans.
Interior view of the first floor.

Lateral view of the house. Sauna.
Kitchen and dining area with mezzanine.

INFORMATION. ARCHITECTS>
KRESINGS ARCHITEKTUR, INTERIOR
DESIGN> LAMBS AND LIONS // 2016.
BOUTIQUE HOTEL> 52 BEDROOMS //
52 BATHROOMS. ADDRESS>
EISENBAHNSTRASSE 17, MÜNSTER,
NORTH RHINE-WESTPHALIA.
WWW.MAURITZHOF.DE

Restaurant and terrace with smooth boundaries.
Detail of the bar. Bedroom in earthy shades. View of
the boutique hotel.

Mauritzhof Hotel

MÜNSTER, NORTH RHINE-WESTPHALIA

The Mauritzhof with its elegant sandstone front and straight alignment could also be found in Milan or Madrid. However, the boutique hotel is located downtown Münster, on the green belt, and it is a gem appealing to aesthetes and cosmopolitans. Upon arrival, you feel at home, as if you are entering the design paradise of a close friend: floor-to-ceiling windows open views into the surroundings, fire flickers in the fireplace, the staff is attentive. The restaurant, bar, terrace, and library all merge to create a platform for encounters. The newly renovated hotel with its 52 rooms focuses on soft contrasts: velvet armchairs, oriental carpets, light fabrics and subdued light meet dark panels, leather furniture and shiny golden accents. Cream, brown, natural and mauve tones soothe and match the soft green of the surroundings. A highlight of the house is the Panorama Suite with a 10-meter window front and a view over the roofs of Münster. You can spend the whole day in and around the Mauritzhof: before having breakfast with organic specialities, you can run in the park, home of some rabbits, to prepare for a meeting in the elegant conference rooms of the hotel. The terrace with a beautiful view along the promenade is a great place to have lunch, the library invites guests to browse, and in the evening the restaurant offers culinary delights made from local products just before exploring the exquisite drinks in the bar. The classy retro-style bar is also a place where the locals meet for a "Münsteraner Sour" drink.

Restaurant with pictures of the local photographer Berthold Socha. Panorama Suite. Detail. Terrace.

GETTING AROUND. WHOEVER IS ON THE WAY IN WESTPHALIA CANNOT DO WITHOUT MÜNSTER. THE CITY IS A VIBRANT PLACE WITH PICTURESQUE GABLED HOUSES, THE PRINZIPALMARKT MARKETPLACE, THE CATHEDRAL, STUDENTS AND CYCLISTS. THE BEST WAY TO EXPLORE THE CITY IS BY A HOTEL BIKE!

INFORMATION. ARCHITECT>
MAX DUDLER, LANDSCAPER>
DR. BERNHARD KORTE // 2016.
MANOR HOUSE> 1,080 SQM //
11 GUESTS // 5 BEDROOMS //
5 BATHROOMS. ADDRESS>
WEINSTRASSE 4, KANZEM AN DER
SAAR, RHINELAND-PALATINATE.
WWW.CANTZHEIM.DE

View from the garden. Orangery.
Common living room with fireplace.

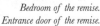
Bedroom of the remise.
Entrance door of the remise.

Cantzheim

KANZEM AN DER SAAR,
RHINELAND-PALATINATE

The late baroque manor house Maison de Wadgasse was built in 1740 for the vineyard of the Premonstratensian monastery Wadgassen. In 2007, Georg Thoma acquired the property. Max Dudler architects renovated the manor house from 2013 to 2016 and added two new buildings to it: the remise and the orangery. Bernhard Korte, landscaper, designed the garden and courtyard. Today the property serves as a guesthouse, an event and cultural venue, as well as the seat of the Cantzheim Winery, founded by Anna and Stephan Reimann in 2016. The main building and the eastern remise contain a total of five guest rooms and an exclusive holiday apartment. The compact and romantic basement with barrel vaulting below the main building includes an event space. The chapel of the house remained completely intact.

The spacious professional kitchen is located in the heart of the manor house, while the orangery, the new building in the west, serves as a room for events and tastings. Its architecture refers to the connection between nature and human culture, which has been expressed in viticulture for thousands of years: elements of glass replace the walls and continue the vertical lines of the vines. On its eastern side, Cantzheim is visually closed off by the two-story shed, built entirely of rammed concrete, with space for two guest rooms.
The spacious gardens, the newly laid-out access road and the farm complex unite the ensemble of buildings.

View of the remise from the garden. A bedroom of the main house. Interior view. Vaulted cellar. Floor plans.

GETTING AROUND. THE GUESTHOUSE CANTZHEIM IS LOCATED IN RHINELAND PALATINATE, EMBEDDED IN A RICH HISTORICAL EUROPEAN CULTURAL LANDSCAPE. IT IS A TEMPORARY EUROPEAN HOME, STARTING POINT FOR TRIPS AND EXCURSIONS TO THE WINE REGIONS OF SAAR AND OBER-MOSEL, TO TRIER, SAARLAND, LUXEMBOURG OR LORRAINE. BEAUTIFUL LANDSCAPES ARE PERFECT FOR CYCLING, CANOEING OR HIKING TOURS. THE LOCATION OFFERS CULINARY WEEKENDS ANDCULTURAL EVENTS AT ANY TIME OF THE YEAR.

INFORMATION. ARCHITECTS>
PETE J.C. WELBERGEN, CLARA
WELBERGEN // 2017. MANOR
HOUSE> 890 SQM // 30 GUESTS //
10 BEDROOMS // 10 BATHROOMS.
ADDRESS> GUT ÜSELITZ, ÜSELITZ 2,
POSERITZ, RÜGEN, MECKLENBURG-
WESTERN POMERANIA.
WWW.UESELITZ.DE

*Interior view of the living room. Library. Top view of
the manor house and its sourroundings. Living
room with open kitchen.*

Gut Üselitz

POSERITZ, RÜGEN,
MECKLENBURG-WESTERN
POMERANIA

Gut Üselitz is located in the south of the island of Rügen in the immediate vicinity of the hanseatic city of Stralsund. The manor house from the 16th century is listed as a historical monument. After the house had fallen into ruins in the 60s, it has now been completely restored. Even if the facts are quickly described the house and the nature in the direct surroundings went through an extremely turbulent history of different uses and deterioration. In 1997 Dr. Astrid von Götz-Welbergen, who later became the owner of the house, and Pete Welbergen, who later became its architect, met this enchanted place. The listed manor park looked rather like a wonderful jungle, and it seemed that the listed manor house could hardly be saved. After the couple acquired the property with the ruins in 1998, the focus was first of all on to secure the remaining rooms. The actual reconstruction did not begin before 2012. From the very beginning, the basic concept of the difficult renovation was to preserve old elements and avoid imitating them, and at the same time to design new elements in a modern way. In the three upper floors of the manor house seven high-quality apartments were furnished, which are available for short- and medium-term stay.

In the ground floor and manor park there are spacious rooms and areas which are at the disposal of all residents, and are also suitable for all kinds of ceremonies, retreats and other events. Uselitz Estate's special feature is its surroundings in the midst of nature that has returned to its natural state.

Entry hall. A bedroom. Ueselitz park.
Bathroom. Floor plans.

GETTING AROUND. ÜSELITZ IS
SITUATED IN THE SOUTH OF THE
ISLAND OF RÜGEN, A WONDERFUL
VAST LANDSCAPE. THE AREA
AROUND ÜSELITZ IS ALSO SPARSELY
POPULATED. THE PROPERTY IS
SURROUNDED ON ALL SIDES BY
THE ÜSELITZER WIEK, A PROTECTED
BAY IN THE SOUTH OF RÜGEN.
SIGHTS IN THE SURROUNDINGS
INCLUDE THE CHALK CLIFFS OF
RÜGEN, THE ARCHITECTURE
AROUND PRORA AND THE
CONCRETE BUILDING OF ULRICH
MÜTHER IN BINZ. IN GARZ THERE
ARE SEVERAL SMALL MUSEUMS
LIKE THE ERNST-MORITZ-ARNDT-
MUSEUM, THE OLDEST MUSEUM
ON THE ISLAND. ESPECIALLY
RECOMMENDED ARE THE THE
SPRING AND SUMMER CONCERT
SERIES.

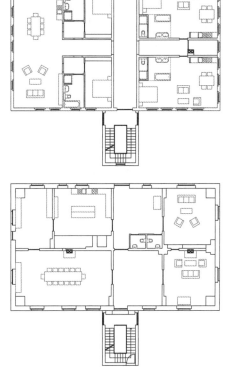

Map of Germany

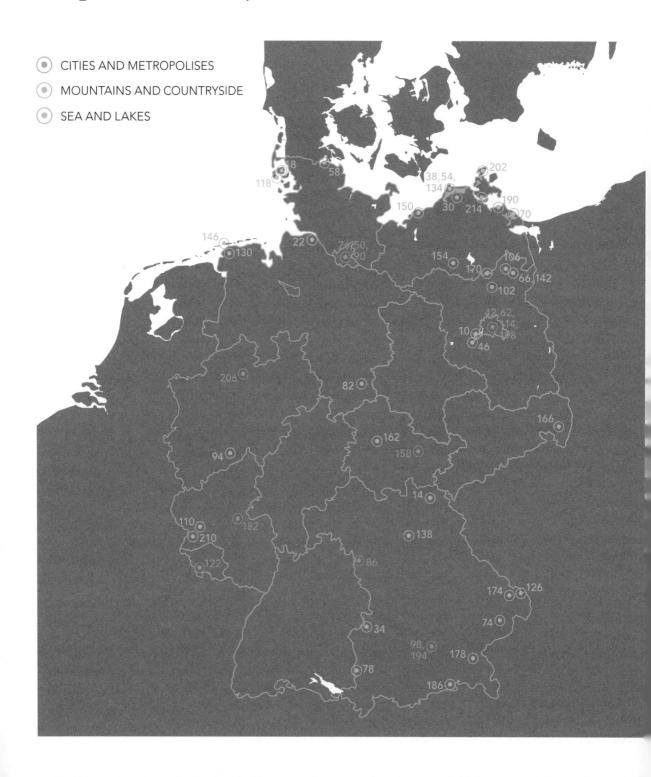

- CITIES AND METROPOLISES
- MOUNTAINS AND COUNTRYSIDE
- SEA AND LAKES

Places to go and things to do

an index of accommodations and activities

CLIMBING

CYCLING

RESTAURANTS

GOLF

HIKING

KAYAKING

SIGHTSEEING

SAILING

SHOPPING

RIDING

SKIING

SWIMMING

WINE TASTING

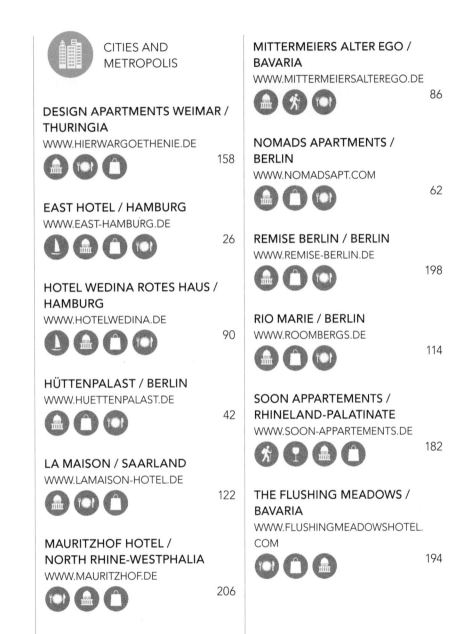

SEA AND LAKES

Picture
Credits

All other pictures were made available
by the architects, designers, or hosts.

Cover front: Samuel Zuder
Cover back (from left to right, from
above to below): Peter Frensemeier, Nele
Martensen, Rainer Hoffmann, Philipp
Obkircher